P9-CKV-426

Essentials of
Project Management

Essentials of Project Management

Clifford F. Gray

OREGON STATE UNIVERSITY

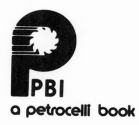

PBI

a petrocelli book

to Mary, Kevin, Robert

Copyright © 1981 Petrocelli Books, Inc.

All rights reserved.
Printed in the United States.
   2 3 4 5 6 7 8 9 10

Designed by Ann Schlesinger.
Typesetting by Backes Graphics

Library of Congress Cataloging in Publication Data

Gray, Clifford F.
  Essentials of project management.

  1. Industrial project management. I. Title.
HD69.P75G7 1981   658.4'04   80-26862
ISBN 0-89433-101-9

Contents

Preface

PROJECT management is concerned with planning, scheduling, and controlling nonroutine activities within certain time and resource constraints. The techniques found in this text for project managers have been tested in thousands of projects and their use continues to grow in every country. These powerful techniques form a total information framework that project managers have found to be simple, practical, and useful in coordinating the diverse aspects of projects and in identifying and solving project problems.

Essentials of Project Management is designed to serve as a complete guide and reference for project managers, trainees, or students of management who search for an understanding of the basic techniques which underlie CPM network-based information systems used in practice. Since the techniques are useful both for small or large projects or organizations, the text should be helpful to all managers regardless of their field.

The focus throughout is on basics and the practical. Manual methods, as well as computer methods, are stressed. Most examples are "synthesized," real-world projects. No background is assumed other than high school mathematics and a slight familiarization with the normal curve used in statistics. One objective of the text is to present the essentials in a simple, straightforward manner so they can be *used* by the average manager. Another is to present only information that is not likely to become obsolete in a few years' time. References have been limited to those "classics" that have made a contribution to knowledge and that have broad applicability in the field of project management. Still another objective is to have the student aspire to certain levels of proficiency. The student should try to develop a *skill* in network logic and planning and in resource scheduling;

that is, he or she should be able to use the techniques discussed in the following chapters in real projects. Further, the student should try to have a healthy *understanding* of cost and control systems, the uncertainty aspects of projects, and computer information systems. This knowledge should be adequate for enabling the student to enter any ongoing project environment and understand the systems involved and the status. Finally, emphasis has been placed on resource scheduling. Experience shows the three major causes of project delays: waiting for materials, poor quality (rework), and resources (labor and equipment) not available at the right time or in the planned quantities. A large percentage of the problems associated with the problem of availability of resources could be avoided if the resources are lined up to meet the plan—something done too infrequently in the real world of project management. It is hoped that the student will develop a keen awareness of the potential pitfalls of failing to schedule resources.

The author expects the text to be used in several pedagogical settings. Selected chapters of the text have been used in approximately 100 executive development programs. The text has been used as a basic text in project-management courses at the college level. It was supplemented with cases, real-world student projects, computer exercises, and literature reviews of the classic and most recent articles. The text has also been used as a supplemental text for specialized classes, such as those in production/operations management, at the senior and the graduate levels. The author further envisions the text as a reference book for project managers and students who wish to reexamine the techniques in view of a new situation or simply to refresh their background of the essentials. Its value should grow with use and experience.

Certain pedagogical features enhance the learning environment. The questions found in each chapter are intended to encourage a questioning attitude and an in-depth examination of the concepts and techniques discussed. Students report that the exercises highlight the use of the techniques presented. Solutions to selected exercises are found at the end of the text. For those teaching project management courses, a teacher's manual is available, which includes suggested answers to chapter questions, answers to exercises, extra quizzes and exercises, true-and-false questions, suggested cases, student handouts, and more than 100 transparencies.

Many people contributed to the development of this book. The most significant contribution belongs to the students at Oregon State University, who originally suggested that class handouts be published in book form.

They assisted greatly in working through the first drafts of chapters and problems. It is a pleasure to give well-deserved credit to the students who provided ideas for chapter problems: Curtis Wolf, Rick Jenness, Gary Margason, and Barbara Sobey. My colleagues Joseph Monks, Charles Dane, and Sang M. Lee read some chapters and offered thoughtful suggestions; their support is appreciated. I am also grateful to Mary Ann Vezzosi who provided professional editorial skill in preparing the manuscript for production. Of course, I assume responsibility for the content of the text. Finally, I wish to acknowledge the favorable working environment and support of the administration in the School of Business at Oregon State University.

This text is dedicated to Mary, Kevin, and Robert, who endured mountains of paper on most tables and chairs in the house for what seems to have been many years. They provided privacy and encouragement when they were needed.

CLIFFORD GRAY
CORVALLIS, OREGON
JANUARY 1981

1
Introduction to Project Management

THE MANAGEMENT of any organization involves the efficient allocation of resources. Space research and defense-related industries have emphasized the term *project management*.

> A project is a complex of nonroutine activities that must be completed with a set amount of resources and within a set time interval. Project management is planning, scheduling, and controlling the complex of nonroutine activities that must be completed to reach the predetermined objective or objectives of the project.

Today's project managers use network techniques to assist them in their tasks—the management science techniques of PERT (program evaluation review technique) and CPM (critical path method). These two techniques are almost identical in methodology; the difference lies in the fact that PERT attempts to handle some of the problems of uncertainty.

PERT and CPM techniques apply to small projects, such as the planning of a neighborhood or fraternal social event, a father and son designing and building a boat, or a heart transplant, as well as to massive projects such as space flights, the development of space stations, the design and construction of a rapid transit complex, and large, corporate mergers. The more complex the interrelated activities of the projects, and the more coordination that is needed, the greater the value of PERT/CPM systems to the project manager. PERT/CPM systems provide methods for measuring actual project progress against expected progress, for comparing consequences of proposed alternative strategies, for predicting future project status, and for optimizing utilization of resources.

1

CHARACTERISTICS OF PROJECT ORGANIZATIONS

Project management applies to small projects managed by a foreman as well as to very large project organizations that include thousands of contractors and workers. It is a useful exercise, however, to identify the characteristics of a large project organization in order to gain an appreciation of the uniqueness of the problems a project manager might face.

Project organizations have distinct characteristics, which mark them as unique from traditional product organizations. Note at the outset that PERT/CPM systems are not applicable to the daily planning, scheduling, and controlling in routine, repetitive product organizations. The production or conversion process in a product organization is repetitive; that is, the process requires repeating the same procedural steps over and over to produce a number of identical items. For example, in a beverage bottling plant or an automobile plant, the nature of work is repetitive; standards for time, quantities, and cost are well established. Conversely, the conversion process in a project organization is *nonrepetitive*; projects are one-time operations or efforts that involve unique problems which occur infrequently. Even though the project manager may depend on past experience and knowledge, every project differs in many specifics from previous ones and thus has its individualized problems. This requires that the project manager respond with fresh approaches to the problems at hand.

Another characteristic found in project organizations is the *cyclical use of resources* in each project. This cycle can be divided into three stages—the design stage, the implementation stage, and the phase-out stage. In the design and phase-out stages, fewer resources (money, equipment, and personnel) are needed than in the implementation stage. Figure 1-1 presents two hypothetical curves that depict this cyclical pattern.

Some examples will clarify the three stages. A consulting firm has been asked to do a study that will project the world demand for wheat for the next ten years. In the planning stage, two or three specialist consultants set up the methodology and sources for collecting the data along with expected project costs and due dates. Next, perhaps ten to twenty source personnel are brought in to implement the study plan which requires collecting the data. Finally, as various sections of the report are completed and tied together, the project is phased out and personnel are moved to other projects.

Another example is a contract to design and build twelve high-speed hydroplane subchasers that will be used to patrol major seaports. In the first stage a few design engineers work on specifications. In the second stage, work is begun on the development and building of the twelve vessels; this involves the use of production facilities, several hundred produc-

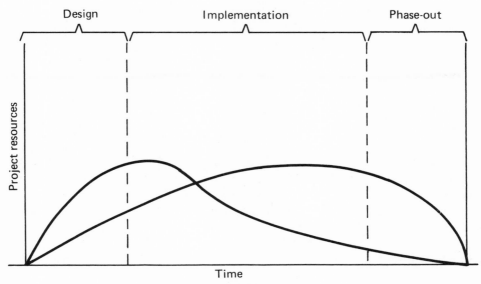

Figure 1-1   Project life cycle

tion workers, and most of the financial resources of the project. Finally, as the eleventh and twelfth subchasers near completion, the project is phased out. Note that in both examples personnel with different skills move in and then out of the project, and that labor requirements are small in the planning and phase-out stages, whereas they are much larger in the implementation stage. It is easy to discern that this project life cycle creates some complex problems of coordinating effort when several different groups or organizations are involved and when several projects are going on simultaneously.

A corollary characteristic to the cyclical use of resources is the *interdisciplinary* nature of project organizations, that is, the use of temporary task forces or teams from all areas within the organization and often from other external organizations to complete the project. General contractors exemplify the interdisciplinary nature of project organizations. For example, a contractor building a high-rise apartment house uses special skill groups within his own organization along with subcontractors who are external to his organization. In the case of the world wheat demand study, wheat and methodology experts were used to design the study, source personnel implemented it, and the project was completed by report writers and wheat experts. Another example was the first landing on the moon in 1969. This required integration and coordination of hundreds of task forces within NASA and over 12,000 subcontractors. The continued work on a near-perpetual source of food for space stations is another example of a project organization that is composed of many diverse organizations and task forces. Clearly, scheduling and coordinating people, money, and materials in such organizations are complex and require that the organization be extremely flexible and capable of reacting quickly to change.

Project organizations usually produce a *limited quantity of output*. For example, the output of the hydroplane project would be twelve subchasers. The output of the consulting firm would be the final report to the client. General contractors usually have several projects in process simultaneously; the total output for such firms in a particular year might be a bridge, a dam, and the installation of the power system for a rapid transit system. Hence, the quantity of output for the project organization is limited, in contrast to that of a product organization.

Since projects are one-time efforts and involve work uniquely different from that of previous projects, time estimates are less certain than they would be in a typical manufacturing plant. For example, the time estimates for building the module used to land on the moon involved more uncertainty than the estimate an industrial engineer would give for building an automobile. This characteristic of *uncertainty of time estimates* creates serious problems in planning, scheduling, and controlling a project.

These characteristics of project organizations—nonrepetitive, cyclical use of resources, interdisciplinary approach, limited quantity of output, and uncertainty of time estimates for activities—emphasize the differences in this type of organization from the typical manufacturing or product organization. These characteristics also dramatize the uniqueness and complexities of the problems a project manager must face.

Again, it should be emphasized that a large formal organization is not a necessary condition to utilizing the PERT/CPM techniques of project management. The scope of project management can range from the management of a small project such as a family doing spring house cleaning to a multiproject aerospace firm or production of a television or movie film.

ORIGINS AND HISTORY OF PERT AND CPM

Prior to the development of PERT and CPM, the most popular technique for project scheduling was the bar or Gantt chart developed by Henry L. Gantt around 1900. These charts show a graphic representation of work on a time scale; see Figure 1-2, which is a hybrid Gantt chart. The primary limitation of this technique is its inability to direct attention to the interrelationships and interdependencies among the many activities which control the progress of the project. In the figure the logical sequence and interrelationships of the activities in the example cannot be determined from the bar chart. Also, this Gantt bar chart suggests that Activity D (Prepare Engine) is behind schedule; this may not be the case. The status of

Activity D is subject to its interdependency with other activities in the project. Although it is possible to redraw the chart to show the interrelationships, the confusion that arises as the size of the project increases soon leads to the abandonment of the Gantt chart method as a planning and control technique. The network techniques of PERT and CPM overcome the interrelationship limitation.

The first pioneering effort to handle the interrelationship—interdependency limitation was undertaken at the E.I. DuPont Company. The management science team of Morgan R. Walker and James E. Kelly set out to study possible computer applications that would assist in planning, scheduling, and controlling engineering projects. Their joint efforts resulted in the Kelly–Walker network technique. In later publications of their work, they referred to the method as the Critical Path Method, CPM. By the middle of 1958, CPM had been tested by DuPont in the construction of a ten-million-dollar chemical plant and in several maintenance projects. CPM was credited with saving DuPont 1 million dollars during the first year it was used. Professional managers recognized quickly the potential and value of CPM. Since its appearance, the technique has been applied to thousands of projects of unlimited variety and size. Interestingly enough, because of the simplicity of the original Kelly-Walker method, it has withstood the tests of time and application; no fundamental changes have been made in the original method.

During the same period that CPM was being developed, management scientists of the Special Projects Office of the United States Navy, of Lockheed, and of the firm of Booz, Allen, and Hamilton were charged with the task of coordinating more effectively the efforts of over 3,000 subcontractors and agencies already working on the development of the Polaris Missile System. In February of 1958 the preliminary draft of the new planning, scheduling, and controlling technique was presented to top management; the technique was subsequently labeled Program Evaluation and Review Technique, or PERT. The cornerstone of this technique (and of CPM) is the use of network methods. By October 1958, PERT was being imposed on the Polaris missile program. It is reported that PERT was invaluable to coordinating the efforts and contractual schedules of the subcontractors and agencies involved. The Special Projects Office credited PERT with slashing eighteen months off the original time schedule and with significant cost savings. Since its original application to the huge, complex Polaris project, PERT has been applied to thousands of projects of unlimited varieties and sizes.

Since both CPM and PERT use network methods to assist in management of projects, what, then, is the underlying difference? Although both management science teams—DuPont and the Special Projects Office—were

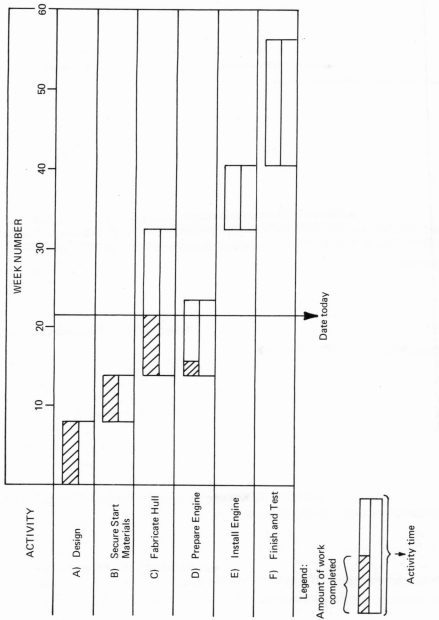

Figure 1-2 Bar chart for subchaser network

charged with similar tasks, they operated in different environments which influenced the outcomes slightly. The CPM team directed its efforts toward construction projects, while the PERT team directed its efforts toward research and development projects. In the construction industry, prior experience with similar projects can be used to predict time estimates for projects within a relatively tight range. However, with research and development projects, a great deal of uncertainty is associated with time estimates because no previous similar experience exists. Thus the PERT team included the probabilistic dimension in its method in an attempt to predict time estimates for each activity in the project and for the total project. Stated simply, PERT assumes the time estimate for an activity lies within the range of earliest time and latest time (for example, between 20 and 30 weeks); CPM assumes the time is predictable or deterministic. In summary, PERT and CPM can each be defined as *the process of employing network techniques to optimize the use of scarce project resources*; selection of the technique depends on the degree of uncertainty associated with time estimates and the costs of missing time estimates.

Although PERT and CPM are the project manager's primary tools, use of them does not guarantee success. Project success depends on the competence of management. The remarkable number of managers reporting how PERT and CPM have contributed to project success, however, vouches for the validity of the techniques when applied to nonroutine projects.

EXPERIENCE WITH PERT AND CPM

The acceptance and the widespread use of PERT/CPM over the years have been phenomenal. The CPM technique has been used successfully by a Colorado hospital to plan open heart surgery; auditors have used PERT to cut audit time; and the Soviet Union uses PERT to plan the entire economy for each year. Product managers have turned to PERT and CPM for new product introductions. The techniques have been used successfully in a multitude of other applications, a representative sample of which appears below:

1. all types of construction
2. first landing on the moon and the space shuttles
3. production of Broadway plays and Hollywood movies
4. overhaul of jet engines and other maintenance problems
5. development of a new business enterprise
6. consulting projects
7. automobile design
8. corporate mergers

9. installation of a computer system
10. off-shore oil drilling
11. planning charity social events
12. product development and marketing
13. solar energy projects

This list barely scratches the surface of the many successful applications of PERT and CPM. Although there have been misapplications, false starts, and excessive expectations of the techniques, the record of success suggests that PERT and CPM are the most significant, practical, and valuable tools yet developed for the project manager.

THE VALUE OF PERT/CPM SYSTEMS

PERT/CPM systems yield most users a return for the extra effort required to use the techniques. The cost of implementing the system has been estimated to range between 0.1 percent to 1 percent of the total cost of an average project. The percentage becomes smaller as the total cost of the project increases; thus on a very large, multimillion dollar project, the cost averages 0.1 to 0.5 percent.* The estimated savings of the average user have been far greater than the costs of implementation.

The savings that result from using PERT/CPM systems take two forms. First, the system forces efficient scheduling of resources; for example, the system reduces the margin of scheduling error; the result is that people, money, and equipment are not idle for long periods of time and *direct cost* savings accrue. Second, the system identifies the critical jobs which control the project completion date. Management can direct its attention to those areas and expedite the project. Any cut in total project time will result in a savings of *indirect costs* such as supervision, interest, taxes, administrative expenses, and other overhead costs. Together, the two types of savings are amazingly significant.

The actual savings derived from using PERT/CPM systems are often difficult to identify and measure precisely, since a project, by definition, is a complex of nonroutine activities. Some firms and researchers, however, have attempted to estimate the time and dollar savings resulting from the use of PERT/CPM systems. The United States Navy noted that the average weapons system contract overruns the agreed original time schedule by more than 36 percent. PERT has been credited with reducing this figure

* Howard Simons, "PERT: How to Meet a Deadline," in *Think*, vol. 28 no. 5 (May 1962), 13–17.

and cutting costs; consequently, many government contracting agencies require some form of PERT/CPM to be used in their contracts. The Catalytic Construction Company used CPM on more than fifty projects and found it reduced both time and cost as much as 25 percent on some jobs. A research firm conducted a survey* of PERT users and found the following results of time saved:

PROJECT TIME SAVED (%)	TOTAL USERS (%)
1–10	43
11–20	41
21 or more	16

Other reports from contractors indicate time savings of up to 25 percent and cost savings of an average of 5 to 15 percent. These figures appear to be remaining constant over time. It seems reasonable to conclude that PERT/CPM systems provide an average time savings of 5 to 20 percent and an average dollar savings of 5 to 15 percent. The benefits suggest the additional effort is warranted where PERT/CPM systems apply.

HOW DO PERT/CPM SYSTEMS ASSIST THE MANAGER?

PERT/CPM systems assist the manager in planning, scheduling, and controlling. It should be emphasized that these functions of the project manager are an on-going process. The world of the project manager is not static—it is dynamic. Therefore PERT/CPM methods require a continual cycle of revision and updating because it is assumed that changes will occur during the life of the project.

Planning

Planning is the process of deciding a future course of action. It involves answering the questions of *what* must be done in the future to reach the project objective, *how* it will be done, and *when* it will be done. PERT/CPM systems answer these questions by construction of a network of the project. This requires that the planner itemize every critical task that must be completed before the project is finished; this "thinking through" of each task almost guarantees management that no activity in the project will be overlooked. These tasks are then linked together in a network which establishes the relationships of all of the tasks to each other and the natural order (sequence) in which they occur.

* Booz-Allen Applied Research, Inc., "New Uses and Management Implications of PERT" (1964).

Questions of How and When are answered by plugging time estimates for each task into the project network. Note that in order to provide a time estimate for each task, the planner must answer the question "how"; that is, before attempting to give a time estimate the planner must decide the methods for accomplishing the task and the level of scarce resources such as people, money, materials, and equipment that will be used for the job. The time estimates for each task along each path (route) through the network are added together. *The longest path through the network is the critical path*, since it controls the completion date of the project. If this planned completion date is not compatible with project objectives, management knows which tasks to expedite, at what cost, and the influence of these changes on the other parts of the project. Since the network establishes the sequence and duration times of activities, the question of "when" an activity will be started is determined. The time estimates provide the basis for setting up an operating schedule.

In summary, the project manager answers the planning question of what, how, and when action will be taken by constructing a PERT/CPM network. The network defines all of the project's critical tasks, stresses the sequence of various sections of the project, presents a graphic picture of the interrelationships among tasks, suggests systematic evaluation of time and cost trade-offs, and provides a basis for determining future work force and other resource needs.

Scheduling

Scheduling is the process of converting a plan into an operating timetable—given resource and time constraints. Although the work sequence and time-oriented network are developed in the planning stage, cost, people, and equipment considerations are usually related to time schedules. PERT/CPM systems provide methods for assisting the project manager in setting up the timetable for the use of project resources. Even in small projects it is possible that the original network plan will require the same resources in two places at the same time. For example, a road builder may find the original network requires a bulldozer tractor on two sites in the same week; or labor skills may be committed to another project and hence not available when called for on the new project. Since only about 15 percent of the tasks in the project control the project's completion time, the noncritical paths in the network allow the scheduler to trade off resources—people and equipment—between critical and noncritical tasks; that is, noncritical tasks can be delayed without influencing the completion date of the project or the logical sequence of activities. If no trade off alternatives are available, the level of resources (overtime, more workers, and more equipment) can be increased to shorten duration times along the critical path. A natural output of a project schedule is an estimate of the completion date of the project.

In summary, project scheduling involves relieving excessive demands on scarce resources and setting up a timetable for the use of these resources. This usually means that the original network must be altered or replanned. PERT/CPM systems assist by scheduling scarce resources used in the project, providing an estimate of the project completion date, and identifying and heading off resource bottlenecks before they occur.

Controlling

Controlling is the process of comparing planned performance with actual performance and taking corrective action where significant differences exist. Continual updating and reporting of PERT/CPM systems present the project manager with a consolidated or summary picture of the current and future status of the project. Deviations from standards are noted; the manager can assess the impact of these exceptions and take appropriate corrective action. PERT/CPM systems assist the project manager by updating and reporting expected versus actual performance and by identifying new critical tasks that may need special attention.

APPROACH AND PLAN OF STUDY

Because the functions of the project manager are planning, scheduling, and controlling, this book is arranged similarly. Specifically, there are chapters covering the management functions and topics important to project managers—computer systems, dealing with uncertainty, and the future of project management.

The planning section includes two chapters. Chapter 2 presents fundamentals and logic of developing project networks. A systematic methodology for computing event, activity, and slack times is discussed in Chapter 3.

The scheduling section adds other dimensions to the time network developed in the planning section. This section discusses the allocation of resources such as dollars, equipment, and labor. Early developers of the techniques recognized the influence cost can have on a project when the schedule is changed to shorten the project duration. The cost dimension is covered implicitly in the planning stage when each activity time estimate is derived because some level of resources (and thus cost) must be assumed in order to arrive at a time estimate for an activity. Early developers also realized the necessity to handle costs in an explicit fashion, so that management could quantitatively evaluate shortening the project by buying time off the critical path. Therefore, PERT/CPM cost-time systems were developed to assist management in assessing the cost of cutting the total project time. These cost-time techniques have undergone changes, variations, revision and synthesis over the years. Chapter 4 covers all these topics.

Setting up an operating timetable for the project resources has become an integral part of scheduling with PERT/CPM techniques. The problem of simultaneous demands for the same resources is a key problem of management. Resource availability and constraints in project scheduling are handled in Chapter 5.

The project performance and control section discusses an integrated network-based information system that can be used to control the project. Chapter 6 presents guidelines for project implementation and offers a framework for cost and key resource control.

Although the text emphasizes the use of manual methods for the techniques, there is a point when projects become so large that computers are necessary. Computers have the ability to digest, compute and generate huge quantities of data rapidly and accurately. These advantages are valuable in large projects. Chapter 7 presents some suggestions for deciding when a computer is necessary and some sample computer outputs.

The next section deals with uncertainty associated with activity time estimates. Chapter 8 discusses the PERT technique which uses three time estimates to compute an average time to perform the activity. Chapter 9 extends the PERT technique by using the Monte Carlo method to capture the dynamic aspects of the project. The simulation model reveals the likelihood of shifting critical paths in the network while the project is still in the planning or bidding stage. This extension is called PERT Simulation.

The final chapter offers some possible changes that seem likely to occur. It suggests that changes in the next two decades will be small and the techniques will largely remain unchanged. Most changes will occur in the computer information systems built around PERT/CPM techniques.

QUESTIONS

1-1. Define the following terms:

project
project management
PERT and CPM
planning, scheduling, controlling

1-2. How do the characteristics of project organizations differ from those of the typical product or manufacturing organization?

1-3. Why do PERT/CPM techniques not guarantee project success?

1-4. What kind of savings can be expected from the use of PERT/CPM systems? What are the possible magnitudes of these savings?

1-5. How do PERT/CPM systems assist the project manager?

PART I
PLANNING

Planning for a project includes listing the activities required to complete the project; establishing the interrelationships among the activities; developing a network; setting activity durations; determining material, equipment, and labor needs; computing activity start, finish, and slack times; and computing the critical path. With this information a tentative plan can be developed. This is also the time when organizational arrangements for the project should be considered. For example, how will authority and responsibility be assigned to ensure the project is completed as expected?

Note that, in the planning phase, time deadlines are not set and resource constraints not imposed. The primary reason for this is to avoid adjustments of the plan (before it is deemed necessary). For example, the initial plan may meet time deadlines and not require any realignment of resources. Trying to outguess possible constraints (and their size) on a complex project is difficult and may result in a movement away from the low-cost efficient plan. Furthermore, premature manipulation of the plan may reduce flexibility in developing a schedule and opportunities to manage when the project is being implemented. If the plan does not meet time deadlines or fit expected levels of resources, a systematic evaluation of time and cost trade-offs can be attempted when developing the schedule—which is the process of setting the project up on a timetable and ensuring the correct quantities of resources will be available *when they are needed.*

The next two chapters cover the standard methodologies used to construct project networks and compute project times. It is important for the student of project management to have a clear understanding of the methodologies found in these chapters, since almost all project scheduling and control techniques in use today depend on the project network and activity times for their data base. Use of these techniques assumes a working knowledge of the project-planning process.

15

2
Elements and Logic
of Project Networks

The cornerstone of critical path methods is the project network.

The network is the graphic flow diagram of the interrelationships, interdependencies, and sequence of all activities and events that must be accomplished to complete the project.

Critical path networks employ only *activities* and *events* as building blocks.

ACTIVITIES AND EVENTS

An activity is an element in the project that consumes time—for example, work or waiting time. Examples of activities are fabricating a pilot model, surveying a roadbed, waiting for cement to cure, setting up account codes, developing publicity, and waiting for legal or management approval. An activity is depicted by a single arrow on the project network. The activity arrow is not scaled; the length of the activity line is only a matter of convenience and clarity, and does not represent importance or time. The head of the arrow shows the sequence or flow of activities. An activity cannot begin until the activities that must precede it have been completed. It is important that activities be defined so the beginning and end of each activity can be identified clearly. This should be done by qualified personnel, since time estimates must subsequently be attached to each activity.

The start and completion of an activity are both called an event. An event represents a specific accomplishment in the project that occurs at an identifiable instant in time. Events indicate the start or finish of one or more activities.

Examples of events are the instant at which a roadbed survey is started, management approval is received, cement is cured, or account codes are established. Note that events do not consume time or other resources. Events are usually represented in the project network by circles called

17

nodes. (The shape of the node can be drawn in any form that is convenient—circle, ellipse, triangle, rectangle, hexagon.) All activity arrows must begin and end with event nodes (see Fig. 2-1).

NUMBERING ACTIVITIES

In constructing networks it is customary to number events to enable easy identification of activities and to indicate the direction of task and time flow. By numbering START and FINISH events of all activities in the network with a pair of unique numbers, each activity can be identified by the start and finish numbers assigned to it. In discussing networks, all start events are referred to as i and finish events as j; see Figure 2-2a. Figure 2-2b shows how the activity might be numbered in the network. The activity can be identified as "Activity 23-30." Note that the start number is smaller than the finish number. This follows the rule for project network diagrams which states that when numbers are assigned to events, the start number should be less than the finish number (i is less than j). This rule eliminates the possibility of "looping" or going backward in time. To reenforce this rule, another rule states that work and time must flow from left to right on the network; see Figure 2-3a. When several activities merge to one finish event in the network, the start event numbers of all merging activities must be smaller than the merging finish event—all of the i's must be smaller than j; see part (c). In part (d), events 74,66, and 83 are all predecessors to event 90. Note that the start nodes 74,66, and 83 are all numbered lower than the finish node number 90; thus it is said they are numbered i less than j. Although numbering events is not absolutely necessary, almost all practitioners in the field use the methods described above to maintain logical sequence within the network. If computers are used, numerical coding is a must; the above procedures will meet all computer requirements for numbering activities.

Although the numbers of the network ascend from the first event to the last, they need not be in a natural sequence (for example, 1, 2, 3, . . . , n). In fact, it is customary when numbering large networks to skip numbers (for instance, 40, 50, 70) to allow for replanning flexibility. Thus, after the initial planning stage it would be possible to insert a forgotten activity or to divide a large activity into smaller segments.

Figure 2-1   Activity and event

(a)   (b)

Figure 2-2   Activity numbering

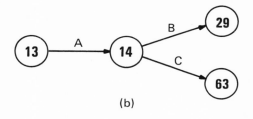

Activity B cannot start until
activity A is completed.

(a)

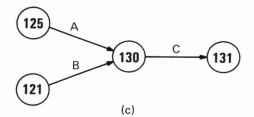

Activity A precedes B & C.
B & C can be done concurrently.

(b)

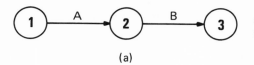

Activity C follows A & B.
A & B can be done concurrently.

(c)

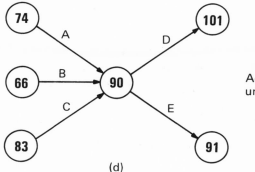

Activities D & E cannot begin
until A, B, & C are completed.

(d)

Figure 2-3   Typical relationships in project networks

INTERRELATIONSHIPS

The completed project network should describe graphically the logical sequence and interrelationships of all the activities which must be accomplished to complete the project. To be certain these conditions are met, three simple questions must be answered for each activity in the project:

1. What activities can take place concurrently with this activity? Or, what activities can be worked on at the same time this one is being performed?

2. What activities precede this activity? That is, what other activities must be completed before this activity can be started?

3. What activities follow this activity? Or, what activities cannot be started until this activity is completed?

Figure 2-3c shows that activities A and B can be done concurrently but that they precede activity C. Asking the three key questions for each activity in the network will avoid errors in network development.

DUMMY ACTIVITIES

In most projects many activities can be performed concurrently or simultaneously. It is possible that two parallel activities could be drawn to have the same start and finish event numbers, as shown in Figure 2-4. This network is incorrect because it breaks the rule of assigning unique numbers to each activity for purposes of identification. Since we wish to avoid confusion and to be able to identify activities by their event numbers, a *dummy* activity is used to alleviate the problem.

A dummy activity is an imaginary activity used to maintain the dependency of one event on another.

Since it is not a real activity, it does not consume time or other resources, nor does it require a name. By convention, dummy activities are represented by a dashed arrow on the project network. Figure 2-5 demonstrates the principle of using a dummy activity for overcoming the problem of parallel activities with identical start and finish nodes (events).

Dummy activities are also useful in linking chain events that are partially dependent. For example, the network planner may set up the activity *blasting* as a prerequisite for *clearing* on a new roadbed. It is possible, however, that some clearing can begin as soon as the blasting crew has moved a safe distance from their original point. By breaking the work packages into smaller segments, and by using dummy activities, it is possible to depict the situation as it actually exists. This is demonstrated in Figure 2-6. The method used in the second example allows for better scheduling of resources—labor, money, materials, and equipment.

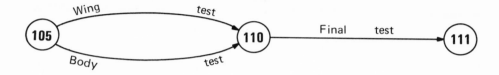

Figure 2-4 Incorrect network for parallel activities

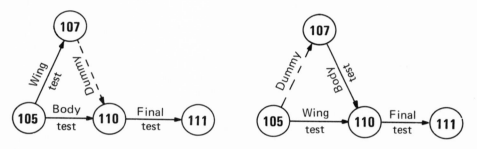

Figure 2-5 Alternative methods for handling parallel activities

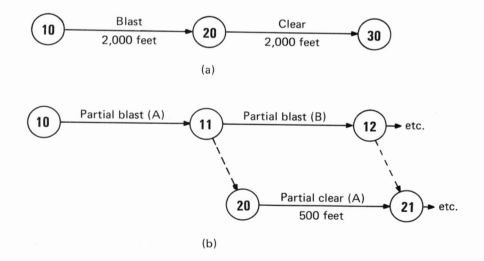

Figure 2-6 Dummy activities for linking chain events

CONDITIONAL STATEMENTS

An additional restraint must be placed on the network designer: conditional statements cannot be allowed in critical path networks. Figure 2-7 represents an illegal procedure. PERT and CPM can only operate under the assumption that all activities will happen and are not conditional. If the conditional statement were allowed, scheduling would have to stop at each conditional statement, and project progress could not be measured.

LOOPING

The last restraint on network design is that of looping. Figure 2-8 schematically demonstrates the loop. An event can occur only once in a project; hence, no path of activities can lead back to an earlier event. In the figure, event 5 would be repeated infinitely; this indicates that some fault exists in the logic of the network. When numerous different people and many departments put together segments of a larger network, the looping error frequently occurs as an oversight. Fortunately, future manipulations of the network will catch looping; but it is best to try to avoid errors and work to reduce the backtracking time required to correct such errors.

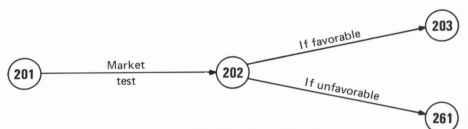

Figure 2-7 Illegal conditional statements

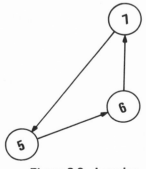

Figure 2-8 Looping

DEVELOPING A PROJECT NETWORK

The adage that a picture is worth a thousand words is even more true when the picture is a project network. The network clearly shows the sequence and interrelationships of all activities in the project. It is the cornerstone to planning, scheduling, and controlling of scarce project resources.

Drawing a project network is relatively easy if the basic rules discussed above are followed. An example best illustrates the process. Let us assume that we wish to draw a network for a construction project in which a prototype cement fishing boat is to be built for a fishing fleet. The construction team meets to develop the project network. First they list all the activities that must be completed before the boat is ready for delivery. Next they answer three questions for each activity in the project: (1) What activities can take place concurrently with this activity? (2) What activities precede this activity? (3) What activities follow this activity?

Most practitioners in the field set up networks by beginning with the last activity and working backward toward the start of the project. Because the end objective or last activity is easily identified, it is a good starting point. The task, then, is primarily one of identifying preceding activities. This approach seems less difficult than identifying the activities that follow one another. Since the outcomes are the same, the user must decide which approach is best.

The summarized results of this process are recorded in Table 2-1. The information in this table is sufficient to draw the initial project planning network. The project network that is derived from the "Network Activity Input Sheet" is shown in Figure 2-9. Note that the sequence and interrelationships are clearly depicted. Responsibility can be assigned and bottlenecks spotted. Coordination becomes easy, and control is facilitated. The network numbers follow the rule that start nodes (*i*) are less than finish nodes (*j*). Observe that the node numbers are ascending but that they are not in a natural sequence; these gaps have been left so more detail can be added later if management wants to do so.

EXTENT OF DETAIL IN THE NETWORK

The question arises in developing every network as to how detailed a network should be. No set of rules has evolved to govern this. Too much detail increases the complexity and cost of the planning and control processes. Some early experiences in the space industry suggest that after a point the marginal return of additional detail decreases rapidly and may even become negative. One firm reduced a network of approximately 20,000 activities to one of about 2,000 to make the network more manageable. The smaller network made general management of the project

TABLE 2-1.   NETWORK ACTIVITY INPUT SHEET.

PROJECT: cement fishing boat

Activity identification*	Description	Predecessors
A	design	None
B	order materials and wait	A
C	prepare engine	B
D	build wire hull frame	B
E	cement spray hull	D
F	install engine	C,E
G	paint interior and install fixtures	E
H	paint exterior	E
I	install accessories	F,G,H
J	launch and test	I

* In simple projects an alphabetical letter can be used to identify each activity.

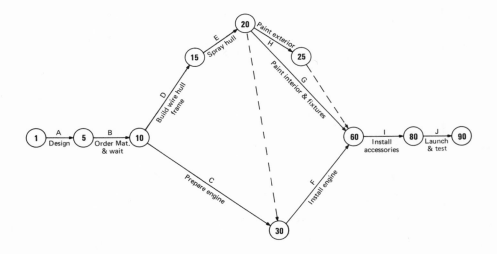

Figure 2-9   Project network for cement fishing boat example

and assignment of responsibility easier for top management.

Of course, it is impractical to draw or show a network with 20,000 activities to be read. Since the optimum number of activities an individual can work with seems to be 100 to 200, a method of subdividing the network is needed. In developing project networks the top-down approach is used to provide each level of management with information needed to manage project resources effectively. Essentially, the top-down approach increases the degree of network detail as the responsibility for completion is assigned for smaller and smaller work packages of the project.

The top-down approach develops in a logical way. When the initial network is developed, it is common to avoid detail so the total project system can be seen easily. This initial total system network usually depicts the major milestones that mark the completion of key events. This macro, or total system, network is adequate for top management. At this point it is possible to bring in middle management to decide where more detail is needed and how much. Any further breakdown of the network into a subnet or fragnet must interface with the total system network. The first-line management level may wish to subdivide a fragnet into even smaller ones. How far to carry this subdividing process depends on many factors, such as project size, familiarity with the type of work, total cost, project duration, and so on. The cement boat example provides an oversimplified illustration of the total system and the subdividing into fragnets. Figure 2-10 shows the addition of the subcontractor's fragnet to the original network in place of the major activity, INSTALL ENGINE. Top management assumed that installing the engine would be the most likely problem area, and they wished to have some method of monitoring the subcontractor's progress. The subcontractor's first-line management may feel the need to break down this fragnet into even smaller subdivisions, or they may accept the fragnet as is and use it for activity scheduling and control.

The key assets of the top-down approach are that each successive breakdown of work packages from the initial total system network does not disturb the logic of the original network, and each fragnet contributes toward final project objectives. In summary, the extent of detail depends on the use of the network and the project itself (see Table 2-2). The best policy to follow appears to be one that includes as much detail as the situation demands—but no more. In this case, experience is the best teacher.

TIME ESTIMATES

After the network has been developed, the time dimension must be added to it. Up to this point efforts have been devoted to the planning process of determining *what* action must be taken to reach the project

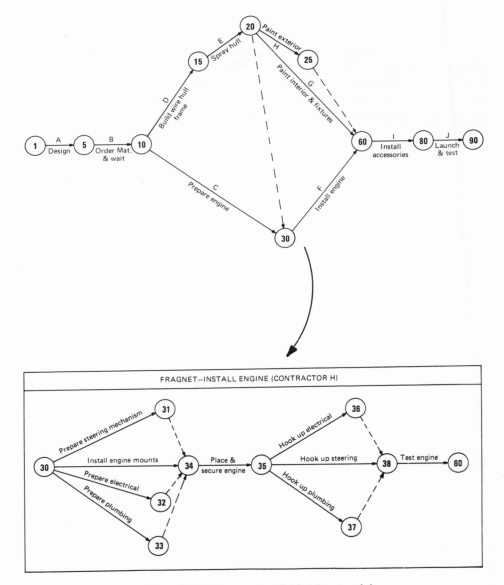

Figure 2-10 Fragnet for fishing boat activity

TABLE 2-2. EXTENT OF DETAIL AND LEVEL OF MANAGEMENT.

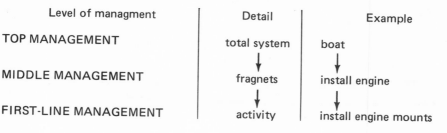

Level of managment	Detail	Example
TOP MANAGEMENT	total system	boat
	↓	↓
MIDDLE MANAGEMENT	fragnets	install engine
	↓	↓
FIRST-LINE MANAGEMENT	activity	install engine mounts

objectives. Each activity in the project has been identified, and the network shows the relationships of all the activities to each other. The next step in the planning process is the gathering of time estimates for each activity in the network. This will answer the question of *when* each action will be taken, as well as providing the basis for developing an operating time schedule for labor, materials, equipment, and money.

Estimating the time required to accomplish a task is difficult when the task is a new and unfamiliar one. No doubt, some error will occur. Some people would suggest that management might be better off not trying to predict activity duration times; but this argument carries little weight. Not attempting to predict duration time means that information already available will not be used. If the task can be performed, enough information exists for determining the activity duration time—even if it is an educated guess. Activity estimates allow management to predict cost and how long it will take to complete the project.

Any unit of time can be used to estimate the activity duration time. The only constraint is that the same unit must be used for the whole network. Workdays and workweeks are the most common units used. A workday could mean an 8-hour day or a 24-hour day; a workweek could be 5 or 6 days. The conditions that *normally* exist should determine the workday or the workweek. If the normal workweek is 5 days, a time estimate of 2.2 weeks means 11 workdays. Activity times are not usually given in terms of calendar dates. Thus, when an activity such as "wait 28 calendar days for legal incorporation" comes up, it is converted to workdays (assume a 5-day week: 28 calendar days = 5/7 x 28 days = 20 workdays). Another similar situation could be the curing of plaster before painting; if this occurred over a weekend, some adjustment must be made to convert the time to workdays. For example, if the plastering is to be completed on Friday night and allowed to cure 3 days, the curing time would be reduced to 1 workday if a 5-day workweek is used. Everyone involved in planning and making time estimates should agree on the meaning of the unit of measure used.

UNDERLYING ASSUMPTIONS OF TIME ESTIMATES

When activity time estimates are given, certain assumptions underlie the estimate. For the planner to provide a time estimate for a particular activity, the planner must decide how the task will be accomplished. Part of this process of deriving the time estimate assumes a certain level and mix of resources—for example, 2 shifts and a crew of 10 or 1 shift and 2 bulldozers. When deriving time estimates for networks, only the *normal* level and mix of resources should be assumed for labor and equipment. Overtime should not be considered unless it is the normal, everyday way of doing business. By assuming a normal network, management will be able to compare (later) the cost of doing the project in ways different than normal; this is discussed in a later chapter, on cost/time trade-offs. The perceptive reader may have already recognized that parallel activities may call for using the same limited resource simultaneously; this apparent conflict will be discussed in the chapter on resource scheduling.

Another assumption that must underlie an activity time estimate is that of independence: setting the time estimate for a specific, discrete activity should not be influenced or adjusted because of some expected outcome in a previous or succeeding activity. For example, the opinion that a breakthrough in design or delivery of equipment will not occur in a preceding activity should not lengthen the time estimate of the activity under consideration. Thus each activity should be considered separately and independently of other activities. This assumption becomes even more significant if the PERT statistical approach or simulation approach is used.

Another assumption underlying the activity time estimate is that "acts of God" are not included in the derivation of the duration time. If events such as tornadoes were included in every estimate, the ability to plan and use resources effectively would be seriously impaired. The time estimate should be as "pure" as possible with no allowances or padding for contingencies which do not normally occur.

The final assumption underlying the single time estimate is that the duration time estimate is the *expected elapsed time*, or t_e. The expected elapsed time is assumed to be an average time and thus there is a 50–50 chance of completing the activity early or late.

THE SOURCE OF TIME ESTIMATES

The degree of success attained with the network planning process is contingent upon the accuracy of the time estimates. Usually those who have responsibility and control over the completion of the activity are the best source for time estimates; this is generally the line supervisor or foreman. There is good reason for this choice. If those responsible for the completion of an activity within a given time constraint participate in making the estimate, they will be encouraged to support and make a commitment to the plan. This follows the management practice of pushing responsibility down the management ladder to those who have direct control over an activity. Participation by those responsible for getting the job done results in many side benefits such as spotting bottlenecks before they occur, finding unexpected problems, answering why some activities take so long, understanding the problems others face, and understanding the individual's role in the total project.

Although it is not generally the case, some situations occur in which the person responsible for completion of the task is not also the most knowledgeable. In such instances two time estimates can be requested—one from the person most knowledgeable, and one from the person responsible. If differences in time estimates exist, they must be explained and reconciled, so that the two parties agree on a time estimate.

A word of caution concerning time estimates and their use: a time estimate is an estimate, and should be treated as such. The expected elapsed time is an average with a fifty-percent chance that the actual completion will take the elapsed time or longer and a fifty-percent chance that it will take the elapsed time or less. Management must be prepared to accept the early or late completion of activities. This is especially true in nonroutine activities that are unfamiliar to the estimator. If the time estimate is used as a club to get things done, management will quickly find that estimators will add a "fudge factor" for their own survival and to avoid later embarrassment. This approach defeats the objective of getting the most reasonable and accurate time estimate possible. Observers in the field have noticed that after estimators have been convinced—by experience—that management is indeed using the time estimate for what it is, the time estimates become more realistic and accurate. Once time estimates are firm, they should not be revised unless there is a change in the level of resources or additional information exists that can make the estimate more accurate (for example, a breakthrough in design or testing). Following such a policy avoids making arbitrary cuts in activity times (for instance, a ten-percent, across-the-board cut in all activities to get the project completed by a specific date). If management wishes to shorten the project duration time, it must secure additional resources and pay the price for the above normal level of resources—for example, overtime—otherwise, quality must be sacrificed. Use of the above management policies greatly enhances the probability of realistic and accurate time estimates.

PROJECT DURATION AND THE CRITICAL PATH

The critical path is the longest path in the network; hence, it determines and controls project duration. If management wishes to shorten project duration, one or more activities on this path must be shortened. If an activity on the critical path is early or late, project duration will vary in that exact amount (assuming only one path is critical). Finding the critical path is important for directing management attention and effort to critical activities where improvement will pay the largest dividends.

Figure 2-11 presents the cement boat example, with hypothetical activity times inserted in the network. (The activity identification numbers have been simplified for convenience.) By definition, the critical path is the sequence of activities in the network that is longer than any other sequence of activities. In this example there are four activity paths in the network. These paths, the expected times (t_e) for each activity, and the sum of the sequence of expected times are given below:

PATH	EXPECTED TIMES	TOTAL
1,2,3,4,5,7,8,9,10	30+20+15+10+5+3+4	87
1,2,3,4,5,8,9,10	30+20+15+10+7+3+4	89
1,2,3,4,5,6,8,9,10	30+20+15+10+30+3+4	112 critical
1,2,3,6,8,9,10	30+20+10+30+3+4	97

In comparing the totals of each path, it is obvious that the sequence of activities in path 1,2,3,4,5,6,8,9,10 has the largest sum of duration times (T_E) and therefore is the critical path. By exception, management can direct its attention to the activities on the critical path.

Other valuable information is now available from the time network. For example, we know that activity 3-6, "Prepare Engine," could be delayed fifteen days ($112 - 97 = 15$) and still not delay the project. This difference between the critical path duration and any other selected path is called *slack*. This kind of information, and much more, is available from time networks.

This method for calculating the critical path is not practical when the project network is more complex. The process of enumerating the activity identification numbers and adding the activity times for every combinatorial path that can occur in the network is a very tedious method for finding the critical path. What is needed is an efficient, systematic method

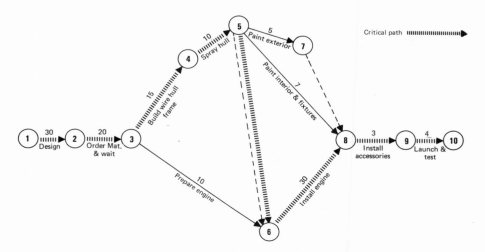

Figure 2-11   Time network for cement fishing boat example

for computing the critical path and gathering other fundamental information to develop an operating time schedule. Fortunately, the developers of the critical path method have provided efficient methods for computing and presenting this information. Chapter 3 presents the orderly computational methods and discusses how the information can be utilized.

QUESTIONS

2-1. Why is networking the cornerstone of PERT/CPM techniques?

2-2. Why are the terms *concurrent*, *preceding*, and *succeeding* important in developing project networks?

2-3. Why should network detail be no more than is necessary and sufficient?

2-4. Why are subnets or fragnets used in developing networks?

2-5. What assumptions underlie an activity time estimate?

2-6. Why is the critical path important to project management?

EXERCISES

2-1. Draw a project network from the following information.

ACTIVITY IDENTIFICATION	PREDECESSOR
A	none
B	none
C	none
D	A
E	B
F	C
G	D,E,F

2-2. Given the information below, draw a project network. Be sure to have a clear ending.

ACTIVITY IDENTIFICATION	PREDECESSOR
A	none
B	none
C	none
D	B
E	B
F	C
G	A,D
H	A,D
I	F
J	E,H,I

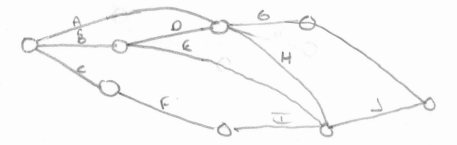

2-3. Develop a project network from the information below. Number your network.

ACTIVITY IDENTIFICATION	PREDECESSOR
A	none
B	A
C	A
D	B,C
E	B,C
F	B,C
G	D
H	D
I	F
J	G
K	E,F,H
L	I,J,K
M	I,J,K

2-4. Draw a project network from the information below. Number your network.

ACTIVITY IDENTIFICATION	PREDECESSOR
A	none
B	none
C	none
D	C
E	A
F	B
G	B
H	D,E,F
I	G
J	G,H
K	G,H
L	I

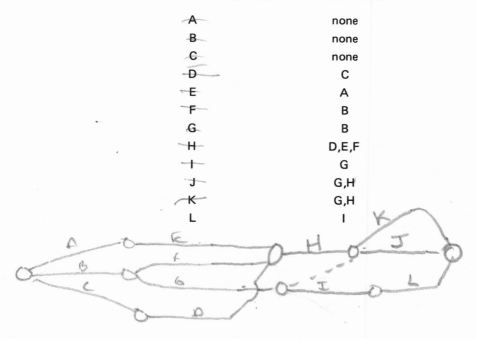

2-5. Below is a list of activities required to consolidate two business firms. Develop the project network.

ACTIVITY IDENTIFICATION	DESCRIPTION	PREDECESSOR
A	codify accounts	none
B	file articles of unification	none
C	unify price and credit policy	none
D	unify personnel policies	none
E	unify data processing	A
F	train accounting staff	A
G	pilot run data processing	E
H	calculate P&L and balance sheet	F,G
I	transfer real property	B
J	train salesforce	C
K	negotiate with unions	D
L	determine capital needs	H
M	explain new personnel policies	K
N	secure line of credit	I,L

2-6. You have decided to write a small book. You believe it will take (1 week) to outline the book. Once the outline is complete, you will begin work on the rough draft; a rough draft should take (7 weeks) to compose. When the rough draft is complete, you can begin writing and typing the final draft; this will take (6 weeks).

One of the most difficult tasks is to find a publisher. You begin this search as soon as the outline is complete; the search can be made while you are writing the rough and final draft, and should be completed in (8 weeks). When you have found a publisher and completed the final draft, the book can be printed. The printing and binding process will take (4 weeks). When the publisher has seen the final draft of your book, he or she will begin to mail advertising brochures to potential customers. This process takes (2 weeks). You can expect your first sale after all of the brochures have been mailed and the printing is complete.

Your book will need a title. You can start to think about a title as soon as you begin the outline. You want (3 weeks) to come up with a title. The title must be selected before the book can be printed.

(a) Set up a project network with the activity times placed above the activity arrows.

(b) What is the elapsed time between starting the book and the sale of the first book?

3
Network Computational Methods and Analysis

IT IS IMPORTANT for project managers to learn and understand the systematic computational approach used in this section to find event, activity, and slack times. The simple networks used for illustration in the text bear little relationship to the complexity found in real-world project networks. The intuitive methods presented in the previous chapter do not do the job in complex networks; in fact, intuitive methods may even give misdirection. For project managers to interpret the results of the manual or the computer-generated event, activity, and slack times, they must have a basic understanding of what the times mean and how they are derived. In special situations and emergencies managers may wish to consider an alternative course of action, which they themselves must calculate rapidly. The importance of learning the basic, manual, computational procedures for project networks cannot be overemphasized.

The definitions and methods of this chapter apply to both PERT and CPM networks. Specifically, the methods are intended to answer two basic questions: (1) How long will it take to complete the project? (2) When can, or must, activities be scheduled? All the computational methods presented here operate on the time dimension of events and activities. For convenience, the computations for events and activities are presented separately; but in reality, event and activity computations are handled together.

EVENT TIME COMPUTATIONS

Event times are important in determining when key events or milestones will occur in the project. The three types of event time are early, late, and slack. Let us examine their meaning and the methods for computing them.

35

EARLY EVENT TIME (T_E)

The early event time for an event is the longest path from the initial project start event to the selected event in the network.

It represents the cumulative time required to reach a particular event. Since computing the early event time requires starting at the project beginning event and cumulating all the individual activity times (t_e) along the longest path or paths to the selected event, the process is called the *forward pass.* Figure 3-1 is a simple network with the earliest event times (T_E) inserted in the symbol near each event node. It is customary to assume that the initial project event will start at time zero. (The time network can be converted to calendar dates when the network computations are completed.)

The early event time (T_E) for a selected event in a series is computed as the early event time for the preceding event (T_{E-1}), plus the activity duration time (t_e). Thus, $T_E = T_{E-1} + t_e$. An exception arises at a *merge*

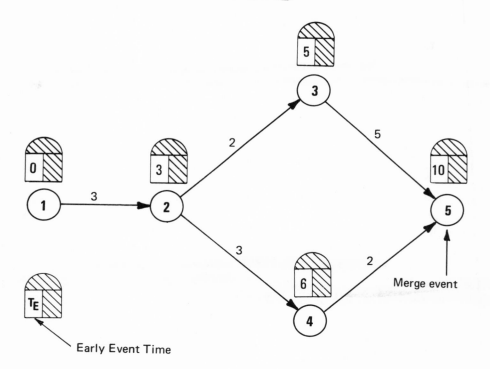

Figure 3-1   Sample network with early event times

event. A merge event exists when more than one path converges to a single event. A general rule, which will cover events in a series or that will merge events, is as follows:

> To compute the early event time, take the early event time of each immediate predecessor event, add the activity time (t_e) of the activity connecting the event, and select the largest value (longest path) leading to the event.

Operationally, this means adding times along each path; when a merge event is reached, the path with the largest time value is selected as the T_E value for the merge event. This rule has been followed in the sample network shown in Figure 3-1. The earliest occurrence time for event 2 is three weeks $(0+3=3)$, for event 3 is five weeks $(3+2=5)$, for event 4 is six weeks $(3+3=6)$. Event 5 is a merge event because it is preceded by the paths formed by events 3 and 4. The earliest that event 3 can occur is five weeks; the earliest for event 4 is six weeks. Hence, the T_E for each path is ten weeks $(5+5=10)$ and eight weeks $(6+2=8)$, respectively. Since ten weeks is the largest value and represents the longest path, the early event time (T_E) for event 5 is ten weeks. This enforces the rule that no event can occur until all activities leading to it have been completed. The computations for the early event times are summarized below:

SELECTED EVENT	PRECEDING EVENT	T_E PRECEDING EVENT (T_{E-1})		ACTIVITY t_e		T_E SELECTED EVENT
1	—	—		—		0 (assumed)
2	1	0	+	3	=	3
3	2	3	+	2	=	5
4	2	3	+	3	=	6
merge {5	3	5	+	5	=	10 } max.=10
event {5	4	6	+	2	+	8 }

The T_E for the final project event is the time required to complete the overall project—ten weeks. This completes the forward pass through the network, since we have examined all paths from the project start event to the end event.

LATE EVENT TIME (T_L)

Computing the latest event time is the reverse of computing the early event time; that is, the process begins with the final project event and moves backward through each path in the network to the project beginning event.

The late event time is the latest allowable time an event can occur and still not alter the occurrence of the project ending event.

Before you can compute the late event time for each event in the network, it is necessary to assign a late event time for the network ending event. Two methods are used for selecting this value. The first entails setting a target time for completion of the project. For example, a target date of 84 calendar days might be set for the completion of the U.S. Exposition at the World's Fair. Assuming a five-day week, this would mean 60 normal workdays ($5/7 \times 84 = 60$) for completion of the project. In this situation the late allowable event time (T_L) for the final event would be set at 60 workdays. The second method for assigning the late event time uses the early event time for the final network event—that is, $T_E = T_L$ for the final event. When a target scheduled time is not available, the early event time for the final network event is assumed to be the latest allowable event date. Use of this method assumes acceptance of the required normal time or the planned project duration time.

After the late event time for the final network event has been selected by one of the methods above, the *backward pass* can begin. This is the process of beginning with the final network event and subtracting individual activity times along each path and branch in the network to the beginning event. The late event time (T_L) for a selected event in a series is equal to the late event time for the succeeding event (T_{L+1}) minus the activity duration time (t_e). Hence, $T_L = T_{L+1} - t_e$. An exception to this occurs at a *burst event*, an event with the tails of more than one activity arrow emerging from it. The formal rule to cover the series and the burst event follows: To compute the latest event time of a selected event,

take the late event time of each immediate successor event, subtract the activity time (t_e) of the activity connecting the events, and choose the minimum (T_L) value.

Stated differently, beginning with the project final event, subtract the activity times along each path for the late event time. When a burst event is encountered, the path with the *minimum* event time value is selected as the T_L for the burst event. The network in Figure 3-2 has the late allowable event times inserted in the symbols near each event.

Note in Figure 3-1 that the early expected time $(T_E = 10$ weeks) was selected for the final event time. In Figure 3-2 the late event time for event 3 is equal to the late time for event 5 less the activity duration time (t_e) for activity 3-5. The late event time (T_L) for event 3 is computed to be $(10 - 5 = 5)$ five weeks. The T_L value for event 4 is $(10 - 2 = 8)$ eight weeks.

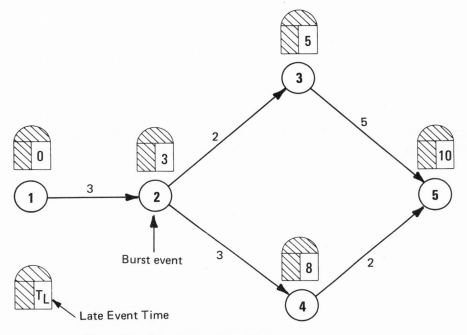

Figure 3-2 Sample network with late event times

Event 2 is a burst event because the tails of more than one arrow emerge from it. In the example two paths emerge from event 2. The late time for event 3 is five weeks; the late time for event 4 is eight weeks. The computation of the late time for event 2 from event 3 is (5−2=3) three weeks, and the computation from event 4 (8−3=5) five weeks. The *minimum* value and T_L for event 2 is thus three weeks. Note that the minimum value comes from the longest backward path. The computations for the late event times are summarized below:

SELECTED EVENT	SUCCEEDING EVENT	T_L SUCCEEDING EVENT (T_{L+1})		ACTIVITY TIME t_e		T_L SELECTED EVENT
5	——	——		——		10 (assigned)
4	5	10	−	2	=	8
3	5	10	−	5	=	5
burst { 2	4	8	−	3	=	5 } min=3
event { 2	3	5	−	2	=	3 }
1	2	3	−	3	=	0

When every event in the network has been assigned a latest allowable event time, the backward pass is complete.

EVENT SLACK

After the early expected and late allowable event times have been computed, the slack can be computed and the critical path identified.

Event slack is the amount of time an event can be delayed without disturbing the completion time of the final event in the network.

Slack may also be called float. Slack identifies areas where project resources can be shifted to make more efficient use of project resources such as labor, equipment, and funds. In other words, since an event should not occur before its early event time nor after its late time, management can schedule the event to occur at any point between the closed interval of the early and the late times. The greater the amount of slack for an event, the more flexibility management has in developing the operating time schedule for resources.

The slack time is computed as the difference between the late allowable event time (T_L) and the earliest required event time (T_E). The equation can be stated as follows:

event slack $= T_L - T_E$

Figure 3-3 presents the sample network with the early and the late event times from figures 3-1 and 3-2 inserted along with the event slack times. The slack computation for each event in the figure is computed thus:

SELECTED EVENT	LATE EVENT TIME T_L		EARLY EVENT TIME T_E		EVENT SLACK $T_L - T_E$
1	0	–	0	=	0
2	3	–	3	=	0
3	5	–	5	=	0
4	8	–	6	=	+2
5	10	–	10	=	0

In this oversimplified example, only event 4 has slack—two weeks. This means that event 4 can occur at any time between workweeks six and eight and not delay the project completion time. Notice the possibility of using this excess time to realign labor resources in the labor schedule.

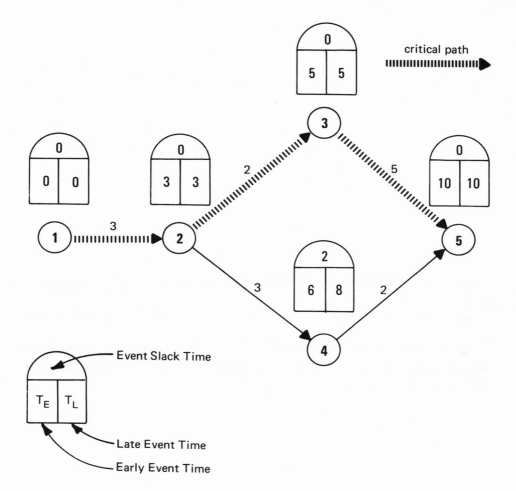

Figure 3-3 Sample network with early and late event times and event slack times

IDENTIFYING THE CRITICAL PATH

The critical path is identified by testing each activity to see if it satisfies three conditions; if the activity meets all the conditions, it is on the critical path. The tests are simple, provided we remember that each activity has a *start* and a *finish* event and each event has an *early* and a *late* event time; Figure 3-4 shows these relationships schematically.

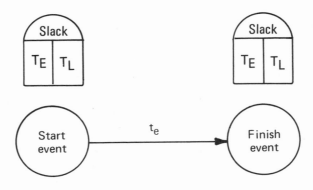

Figure 3-4   Activity and event times

The three test conditions (assuming final project event $T_E = T_L$) are as follows:

1. The early and late event times of the start event must be equal: $(T_E = T_L)$.
2. The early and late event times of the finish event must be equal: $(T_E = T_L)$.
3. The difference between the early event time for the finish event and the early event time for the start event for an activity must equal the activity duration time.

The uninitiated often overlook the last condition. A simple example can demonstrate the importance of this condition. It is common to say that events having zero slack form the critical path of the network. This is true, but problems of interpretation can arise. How would you interpret the network illustrated in Figure 3-5? Observe that each activity meets the first two conditions but that activity 1-3 does not meet the third ($9-3 \neq 3$). Actually, activity 1-3 is not on the critical path, and it can start at any time between zero and six days. In actual practice, the situation depicted in this figure occurs in almost all large projects.

Test the activities in the network shown in Figure 3-3 to find the critical path. Each activity on path 1,2,3,5 meets all of the conditions and thus identifies the critical path. Since the critical path has zero slack, there is no flexibility in scheduling resources; that is, events 1,2,3,5 must occur at their earliest times or the project will not be finished as planned—if one of these events is delayed, the whole project will be delayed. The example network in Figure 3-3 is simple, and the critical path is obvious; but this will not

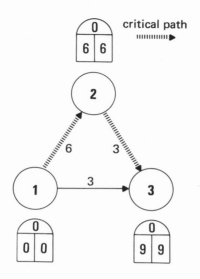

Figure 3-5   Identifying the critical path

be the case with larger networks. Complex networks may have two or more critical paths. The systematic procedures described above will identify event times, slack, and the critical path in any project regardless of size or complexity.

SCHEDULED COMPLETION TIMES AND EVENT SLACK

When there is a scheduled completion time (T_S) for the project, the late event time for the final event is set equal to the scheduled time—that is, $T_L = T_S$. The slack for the final event can be zero, positive, or negative. If the scheduled completion time should happen to be the same as the earliest event time (T_E) for the final event, the slack would be zero. If the T_S is greater than the final T_E, then the slack will be positive. If the T_S is less than the final T_E, the slack will be negative. If a difference exists between the scheduled time and the early event time for the final event, this value (constant) will be the same value found at each event along the critical path. Hence, the critical path is identified by finding the path with the lowest (least) constant slack value. The activity test for the critical path discussed above still applies except that conditions 1 and 2 are modified slightly. If early and late event times for the start and finish events of the activity are not equal—$T_E \neq T_L$—they will differ by the constant slack value found at the final project event. Figure 3-6 illustrates the impact of a scheduled time of ten weeks imposed on a hypothetical project. The critical path is

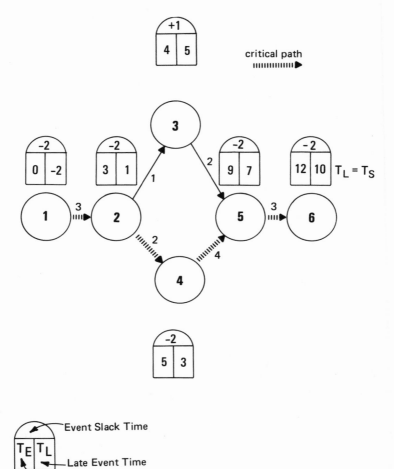

critical path

Event Slack Time

Late Event Time

Early Event Time

$T_E | T_L$

$T_L = T_S$

Figure 3-6 Network with scheduled completion time

identified by finding the path with the constant slack value $(T_S - T_E)$ found at the terminal event 6. The slack values for the network are listed below:

SELECTED EVENT	LATE EVENT TIME T_L		EARLY EVENT TIME T_E		EVENT SLACK $T_L - T_E$
6	10	–	12	=	–2
5	7	–	9	=	–2
4	3	–	5	=	–2
3	5	–	4	=	+1
2	1	–	3	=	–2
1	–2	–	0	=	–2

The slack value at event 6 is negative two weeks. The critical path can be identified by finding the path in which the events carry the negative slack of minus two weeks; this is path 1,2,4,5,6. Note that the early expected event times do not change; they are based on activity time estimates of the *required* time to complete the work packages. In projects where the slack on the critical path is negative, management will probably resort to adding more resources to get the project finished as scheduled—for example, working overtime, finding a new method for doing the work package, or finding a way to make series activities parallel. In practice, where large projects must be monitored, scheduled dates are imposed on key milestone events that could be located almost anywhere in the network—not just at the final event.

The computations thus far have been on network events. We have learned how to calculate the early and late event times and event slack. The early event time is important because it tells management the *required* time to reach an event and to complete the project. The late event time is significant because it tells management the latest *allowable* time an event can occur without delaying the project. Slack gives management an indication of the degree of flexibility on a path; path flexibility is tremendously important in actual scheduling of labor and equipment resources. Slack is so important that it is customary to develop slack charts, which rank events and activities by their slack. These charts begin with events or activities that have the least slack and end with the event or activity with the most positive slack. Management would then direct more attention to those work packages with the least slack, since any delay in them (greater than their slack) would cause a delay in the project. Slack is also used to assign labor and equipment when two activities in the network demand the same resource at the same time. If the activity on one path has a large positive slack value, it may be possible to delay the work on this activity to allow the work on a more critical activity to be completed first. This problem is discussed again in the next section, on activity computations, and in the chapter on resource scheduling.

Event analysis tends to be path-oriented; this is useful to top management in monitoring the progress of the project. Most of the major problems in projects, however, lie in scheduling the scarce project resources to specific *activities*—seeing that work packages are done on time. Therefore, we shall now turn our attention to activity start and finish times and to activity slack. Much of what we have already learned about events will be useful in activity computations.

ACTIVITY TIME COMPUTATIONS

This section deals with the question, When can, or must, activities be scheduled? The answer is constrained by the computed early and late activity times. These times set boundaries on the amount of movement that can take place in scheduling activities without affecting the project completion date. The format used in computing event times will be used in computing activity times; that is, we will calculate the early activity times in the forward pass, the late activity times in the backward pass, then determine the slack values for each activity. The four activity times used in the forward pass and the backward pass are defined below for computation purposes:

FORWARD PASS

early start (ES):   the earliest time an activity can start if all the connected predecessor activities are started as early as possible; or, the early event time (T_E) of the activity's start event

early finish (EF): the early start for the activity, plus the time required to complete the activity

BACKWARD PASS

late finish (LF):   the latest time an activity can be finished if all the connected succeeding activities are finished as late as possible; or the late event time (T_L) of the activity's finish event

late start (LS):   the late finish time for the activity, less the time to complete the activity

FORWARD PASS

The forward pass for activities is similar to the forward pass for events; that is, we are dealing with the *early* activity times. When scheduling activities, it is valuable to find the early start (*ES*) and early finish (*EF*) times for each activity. These times are used in scheduling work packages.

The process of computing these times is best illustrated with an example. Figure 3-7 presents the network from the cement boat example, with all the times inserted. The early start time for the first activity (1-2) is customarily set at zero time. The early start for each following activity is found by adding the activity times along each path. When a merge event is encountered, the path with the largest time is used as the *ES* time for all the activities emerging from this event. Some readers have recognized that the early event time (T_E) at the tail of the arrow is also the early start time for the activity. Since you already know how to compute early event times and these times equal the early start times, only the early finish times remain in the forward pass. The *EF* for an activity is simply the early start for the activity (or early event time T_E) plus the activity duration time (t_e). The equation is:

$$EF = ES + t_e$$

or

$$EF = \text{start event } T_E + t_e$$

The early finish time for each activity is customarily inserted at the *head* of the arrow. For example, the *EF* for activity 3-6 is 60 days (50+10=60); this figure is inserted at the head of the activity arrow. When all of the early start and finish times have been found, the forward pass is complete.

BACKWARD PASS

The backward pass for activities computes the latest allowable start and finish times for each activity. Before the computations can begin, the latest allowable event time for the final project event must be selected; unless a scheduled time is specified, it will always be set equal to the early expected event time for the final project event. In the cement boat example in Figure 3-7, the early event time of the final project event is 112 days; thus $T_E = T_L = 112$ days. We learned from the forward pass that the early expected event time is also the early activity start time for activities emerging from the event. A similar situation occurs in the backward pass. The latest allowable *event* time at the head of the arrow is also the late finish time for the activity. For example, in Figure 3-7 the late finish time

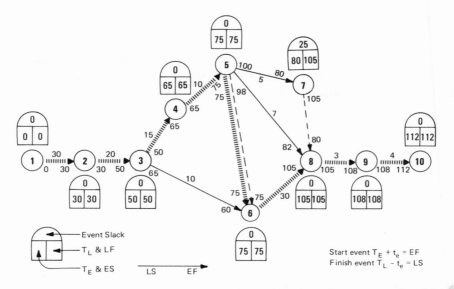

Figure 3-7 Cement boat network with early and late times for events and activities and event slack times

of activity 2-3 is 50 days and of activity 3-6, 75 days. Because the late event time at the head of the arrow is also the late finish time for the activity, the late activity start times are the only times left to compute for the backward pass. The late start time for an activity is the late finish time for the activity less the activity duration time. The equation is shown below:

$$LS = LF - t_e$$

or

$$LS = \text{finish event } T_L - t_e$$

For example, the late start for activity 4-5 is 65 days (75−10=65); for activity 5-7 the late start is one hundred days (105−5=100). Observe that the late activity start time is placed at the *tail* of the arrow. When the late start times for all activities have been computed, the backward pass is complete.

Now that methods for computing event activity times have been discussed, it is important to note again that, in actual practice, the process of computing event and activity times is not separated. In practice, you move from one activity to the next, computing both activity and event times.

For example, at a merge event the early finish times for each merging activity must be known in order to select the largest time value for the early event time for the merge event. The computations were presented separately only for ease of exposition and learning.

ACTIVITY SLACK AND THE CRITICAL PATH

Activity slack (float) is more significant than event slack because it is the manipulation of activity slack that permits flexibility in scheduling specific work packages. A noncritical activity, for instance, can be delayed (equal to total slack) without influencing the project completion time. The larger the slack value, the greater the flexibility.

This section deals only with total activity slack, which is most practical for scheduling resources. Total activity slack is sometimes called primary float (slack). Total activity slack is defined as

the amount of time an activity can be delayed without disturbing the finish time of the project. Total slack is computed as the difference between the late and early activity start or finish times.

It can be stated symbolically as follows:

activity slack = $LS - ES$ (LS for the activity - start event T_E)

or

activity slack = $LF - EF$ (finish event $T_L - EF$ for the activity)

Total activity slack represents the amount of time the scheduled start or completion of the activity—or a combination of both—can be altered without disturbing project completion time.

The computed activity slack times will be inserted in a "project worksheet" that is sometimes used in place of drawing a network. The rationale for preparing a worksheet instead of a network is that eventually the network information must be summarized in list form for scheduling activities anyway. Another reason given is that the network soon becomes cluttered with numbers and the confusion index can become quite high. Such reasons are valid; but the value of drawing the network and at least calculating the activity and event times outweighs the suggested efficiency of using a worksheet and no network. The network is invaluable in coordinating the efforts of different groups, in seeing that no activity in the project has been left out, in marking progress, and in easing the difficulty of computing activity and event times. Hence, practitioners who must do all the computations manually usually draw the network, compute activity and event times on the network, transfer these times to a project work-sheet, and compute the activity slack time on the worksheet. The results of following this procedure with the cement boat example are presented in the project worksheet, Table 3-1.

Some examples will illustrate the activity slack computation. Activity 1-2 has zero slack because it is on the critical path; the activity slack is computed as the late activity start minus early start which is zero $(0-0=0)$ or late finish minus early finish, which is also zero $(30-30=0)$. Activity 3-6 is not on the critical path and thus slack is positive fifteen days $(65 -50=15$ or $75-60=15)$. The slack for the other activities is computed in a similar manner.

Of course, if the slack is used up on an earlier activity in a series, more slack cannot be used on subsequent activities in the series even though each activity in the series has the same amount of slack. For example, in Figure 3-8 two activities in a series are presented along with their respec-tive event and activity times. Activity 5-6 and activity 6-7 both have slack of 30 days—$90-60=30$ and $110-80=30$, respectively. If the start of ac-tivity 5-6 is delayed until day 90, the slack for the path is used up and is not available again for activity 6-7. The key problem with slack is deter-mining where it can best be used. One method for getting an overview of the degree of flexibility in the noncritical slack paths is to list all the ac-tivities in the network in the order of increasing slack. Such a ranking al-lows management to direct attention to the activities with the least slack. Slack is also the means by which resources are balanced in situations where different tasks compete for the same scarce resources. Chapter 5 is devoted to the problem of resource leveling or balancing.

The critical path can still be found by satisfying the three conditions given in the event section of this chapter. If you are working off the pro-ject worksheet, however, the critical activities can be found simply by identifying those activities with zero slack (see Table 3-1). Note that the three conditions hold for each activity on the critical path.

Two other ancillary topics should be dealt with before a chapter on "methods" is complete, however. Some recognition of other network dia-gramming methods should be given because a great deal of freedom is exercised in practice in network diagramming. Another topic that has been skirted to avoid confusion in understanding the fundamentals is calen-dar dates. Before bids or schedules can be considered, the network figures must be converted to calendar dates. Let us deal with each topic in greater detail.

TABLE 3-1.

PROJECT WORKSHEET cement boat project

Activity identification number	Activity description	Duration t_e	Early		Late		Total slack	Critical path
			Start (ES) (T_E start event)	Finish (EF) ($ES + t_e$)	Start (LS) ($LF - t_e$)	Finish (LF) (T_L finish event)	$LS-ES$ or $LF-EF$	
1-2	design	30	0	30	0	30	0	x
2-3	order material and wait	20	30	50	30	50	0	x
3-4	build wire hull frame	15	50	65	50	65	0	x
3-6	prepare engine	10	50	60	65	75	15	
4-5	cement spray hull	10	65	75	65	75	0	x
5-6	dummy	—	75	75	75	75	0	x
5-7	paint exterior	5	75	80	100	105	25	
5-8	paint interior and fixtures	7	75	82	98	105	23	
6-8	install engine	30	75	105	75	105	0	x
7-8	dummy	—	80	80	105	105	25	
8-9	install accessories	3	105	108	105	108	0	x
9-10	launch and test	4	108	112	108	112	0	x

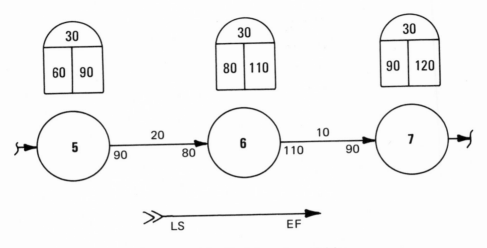

Figure 3-8 **Slack in series activities**

OTHER NETWORK DIAGRAMMING METHODS

Many ingenious schemes exist for manually drawing networks and designating event, activity, and slack times. Two other frequently used schemes, presented in Figure 3-9, are common where manual methods are used. In part (a) squares and triangles represent early and late event times, respectively; the reverse of triangles and squares is also used frequently in practice. Part (b) presents a method reported by Moder and Phillips. This method has the advantage of getting all the needed scheduling information on the network. Other schemes have been developed to identify milestone events; although no general standards appear to be emerging, almost all approaches modify the shape of the event node, for example, a milestone node is often drawn as a hexagon. Special symbols have also been developed to identify events which interface with fragnets. In the case of milestone and interface events, a potpourri of symbols exists; each project group has developed its own set of symbols. The practitioner must make his or her own choice of symbols.

Another approach to drawing networks is the activity-on-node precedence system. This approach places the *activity* within the node circle or square; the arrows are used only to show dependencies and do not represent time. The activity-on-node approach eliminates the dummy activities and events and does not accommodate fragnet systems. For some large projects where events are used for marking project progress and management control (for example, milestone events), eliminating the event turns

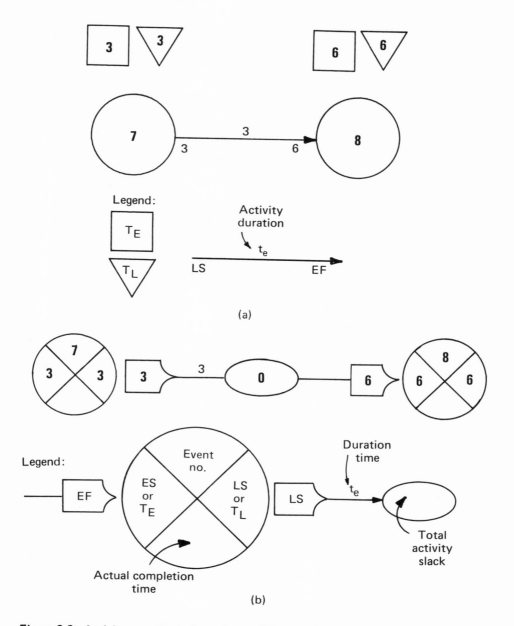

Figure 3-9 Activity-event notation schemes (The symbols used in part (b) are adapted from *Project Management with CPM and PERT*, 2nd edition, by Joseph J. Moder and Cecil R. Phillips. © 1970 by Litton Educational Publishing, Inc. Reprinted by permission of Van Nostrand Reinhold Company.

out to be a significant disadvantage. Many smaller projects, especially construction projects, place emphasis on the activity work package; in such projects the activity-on-node approach is attracting a small but growing group of followers. Computer programs have been developed to assist this group. Figure 3-10 presents a synthesized network for installing a data processing system which uses the activity-on-node scheme. The scheme for arranging the activity times around the activity node is a manual method suggested by Moder and Phillips. This scheme places the activity times in an easily understood order.

An additional network scheme allows the planner to use more options in expressing dependency relationships that might exist between activities. Figure 3-11 presents examples of the schematic format used by IBM in their project control manuals. Part (a) depicts the standard relationship found in activity-event networks (see Fig. 3-7) and activity-on-node networks (see Fig. 3-10); in other words, the start of activity B depends on the finish of activity A.

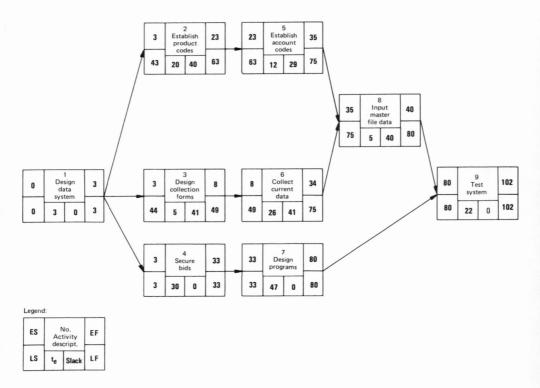

Figure 3-10 Activity-on-node scheme: installing a data processing system

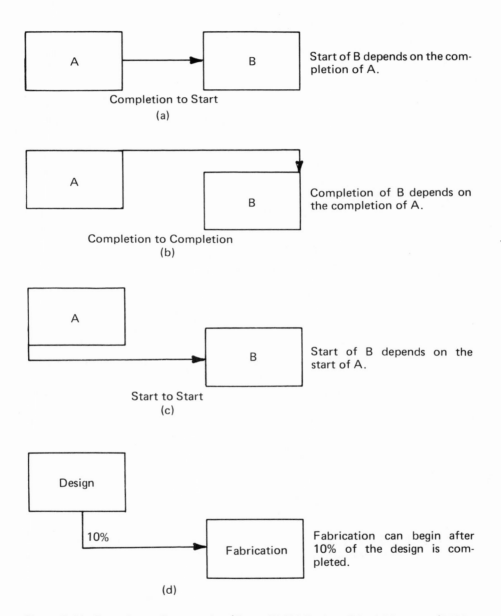

Start of B depends on the completion of A.

Completion to Start
(a)

Completion of B depends on the completion of A.

Completion to Completion
(b)

Start of B depends on the start of A.

Start to Start
(c)

Fabrication can begin after 10% of the design is completed.

(d)

Figure 3-11 Precedence diagramming (From "1130 Project Control System (1130-CP-05X) Program Description Manual," No. H20-0342-1 (White Plains, N.Y.: IBM Corporation, 1968), pp. 18–19.

Part (b) shows a completion to completion relationship in which the completion of activity B depends on the completion of the preceding activity A.

Part (c) depicts the start-to-start relationship in which the start of activity B depends on the start of the preceding activity A. This relationship is especially useful in projects characterized by "ladders" or step-parallel paths. Precedence diagramming also allows the planner to extend the start-to-start and completion-to-completion concepts and specify the *lag* time that must occur before the next activity can be started or completed. This opportunity for the planner to deal with a portion of the activity more closely resembles the true situation found in practice.

Part (d) of the figure presents an example of the use of the time lag feature in a start-to-start situation. This part is interpreted as follows: fabrication can begin when 10 percent of the design is completed. Time units can be used in place of percentages, for example, the lag could be expressed as 1.5 weeks. If regular networking techniques are used in situations such as "design," the activity would have to be broken into smaller activities which would result in more activities on the network. Evidence would suggest that precedence diagramming will be used more in the future because of the flexibility offered in diagramming relationships closer to those that are found in practice. It is not likely, however, that precedence diagrams will replace the standard activity-event network completely. In projects with several merge and burst events, the dependency arrows in precedence diagramming can soon reach a point where they actually add confusion. Furthermore, precedence diagramming does not facilitate the use of fragnets and eliminates events; for many projects, both fragnets and events are desired for monitoring progress.

CALENDAR DATES

At some point in the planning process the general time network must be converted to calendar dates. When the conversion is done manually rather than by a computer, the workdays of the network must be converted to calendar days. The workday calendar does not include weekends, holidays, and other days that are not normally scheduled workdays. Development of calendar dates simply means beginning with a calendar start date and extending workdays and nonworkdays on the calendar until the workdays are exhausted. For example, a project that starts on January 1 and has a duration of 240 workdays would have a calendar completion date close to December 31 of the same year. Care must be exercised in interpretation of calendar schedules. If an activity is due for completion on

August 23, it need not be completed until the *end* of the workday on August 23. Table 3-2 presents a segment of a hypothetical project in which a five-day week is assumed. Allowance must be made for calendar waiting times which take place during a weekend or a holiday. For example, cement laid on Friday will cure over the weekend; thus an allowance must be made to the activity cure time since it occurs on days that are not normally workdays. In this case, the cure time would have to be shortened two workdays. Most computer programs have routines that automatically print out calendar dates. All that is needed is a project start date and the duration of the workweek.

TABLE 3-2. WORKDAY CALENDAR.

	start date Sept. 1
Calendar date	Project workday
Sept. 1	1
2	—
3	—
4	— (Labor Day)
5	2
6	3
7	4
8	5
9	—
10	—
11	6
.	.
.	.
.	.

SUMMARY

The purpose of this chapter has been to develop manual methods for gathering planning, scheduling, and analysis inputs. We can now answer the questions of how long the project will take and when activities can and must start if they are to be finished as planned. A thorough understanding of the fundamentals and techniques of this chapter will provide a sound basis for extending one's knowledge in project management, for interpreting any network found on the job, and for developing a sound plan and schedule for the efficient use of project resources.

BIBLIOGRAPHY

Abernathy, W.J. "Subjective Estimates and Scheduling Decisions." *Management Science*, Vol. 4 no. 2 (Oct. 1971) B80–88.
Kidd, J.B., and Morgan, J.R. "The Use of Subjective Probability Estimates in Assessing Project Completion Times." *Management Science*, Vol. 16 no. 3 (Nov. 1969) 266–69.
King, William R., Wittevrongel, Donald M., and Hezel, Karl D. "On the Analysis of Critical Path Time Estimating Behavior." *Management Science,* Vol. 14 no. 1 (Sept. 1967) 79–84.

QUESTIONS

3-1. The early time for a merge event is the longest path leading to it. Why does this rule exist?

3-2. Why is slack said to be one of the most important concepts of project management?

3-3. Why does the use of the slack of any activity along a path preempt its use on a succeeding activity on the same path?

3-4. Why is negative slack possible even before the project begins?

EXERCISES

3-1. Given the network below, compute the event and activity times on your network. From the network, fill in a chart similar to the one shown below.

	EVENTS				ACTIVITIES				
	ET	LT	Slack		ES	LS	EF	LF	Slack
1	___	___	___	1-2	___	___	___	___	___
2	___	___	___	1-3	___	___	___	___	___
3	___	___	___	1-4	___	___	___	___	___
4	___	___	___	2-5	___	___	___	___	___
5	___	___	___	3-5	___	___	___	___	___
				4-5	___	___	___	___	___

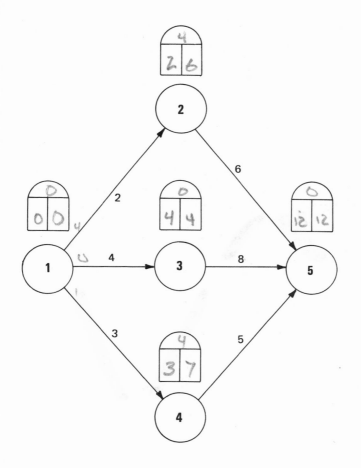

3-2. A project network is presented below. Compute the times for each event and activity listed, and identify the critical path.

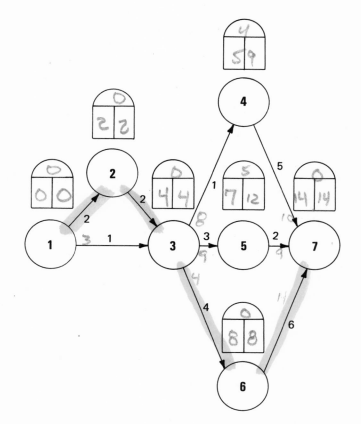

3-3. Compute the early and late start and finish times for each activity and event in the project network below. Identify the critical path.

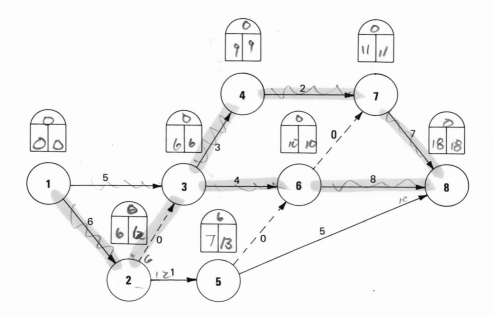

3-4. Complete the following table:

ACTIVITY	DURATION	ES	LS	EF	LF	SLACK
1-2	3	0				
1-3	5	0				
2-3	0	6				
3-4	1					
3-5	2					
3-6	4					
4-7	3					
5-6	0					
5-7	6					
6-7	5					

3-6
6-8
8-12

3-5. Compute the activity times for each activity listed:

ACTIVITY	DURATION	ES	LS	EF	LF	SLACK
1-2	4	0	-2	4	2	-2
1-3	2	0	0	2	2	0
1-4	6	0.	2	6	8	2
2-3	0	4	2	4	2	-2
3-6	3	2	2	5	5	0
3-8	1	2	9	3	10	7
4-8	2	6	8	8	10	2
6-8	5	5	5	10	10	0
8-10	3	10	11	13	14	1
8-12	4	10	10	14	14	0
10-12	0	13	14	13	14	1

3-6. Based on the information below given to us by the project planner about marketing a new product, do the following:

(a) Draw a network showing early and late start times for each event.
(b) Number the network.
(c) For each activity compute the early and late start, early and late finish, and slack times.

ACTIVITY ID	DESCRIPTION	ACTIVITY PREDECESSOR	ACTIVITY TIME
A	staff	None	2
B	develop market program	A	3
C	select channels of distribution	A	8
D	patent	A	12
E	pilot production	A	4
F	test market	E	4
G	ad promotion	B	4
H	set up for production	D,F	16

3-7. Antarctic Expedition: A scientific expedition to the Antarctic is being planned. The person in charge of this expedition knows it takes (3 months) to develop a preliminary plan and have it approved. Once the proposal is approved, it takes (3 months) to draw up the detailed scientific plan and coordinate it with other research being done in the area. As soon as the detailed plan is complete, personnel can be hired. The hiring process takes (2 months). Indoctrination of the personnel for this expedition will take (1 month) and can begin as soon as they are hired. Plane reservations, passports, and shots for members of the expedition can be arranged at the same time as the indoctrination and will require (2 months) to obtain. Special equipment will be required for this expedition. Once the detailed plan is complete, it will take (1 month) to select the equipment to be used. It is then necessary to see if this equipment is already available in the Antarctic. This process takes (6 months). It will then take an additional (3 months) to obtain all equipment which is not available in the Antarctic (it is a certainty that some equipment will not presently be there). After the equipment arrives, it must be tested. Technical personnel can do this testing when they have completed their indoctrination. The testing takes (2 months).

Special clothing is also necessary. It takes (5 months) to obtain this expedition gear. The order for this can be placed as soon as all the personnel have been hired. As soon as the clothing arrives and upon completion of the equipment testing, these items can be shipped to the Antarctic. It takes (3 months) for materials to reach the Antarctic. The equipment must be in the Antarctic by the time the expedition team leaves Seattle for their flight to New Zealand and the Antarctic.

Assignment:

1. Draw the network for this project.
2. Compute the early and late start times, early and late finish times, and slack time for events and activities.
3. Locate the critical path.

3-8. Marketeers, Inc.: Top management of Marketeers, Inc. has recently decided to enlarge their product line. The new product is to be an item that is unique and that will appeal to a large segment of your consumer market. As product manager, you have been assigned the responsibility of coordinating this project, from the selection of the new product through its distribution.

The first problem confronting you is the selection of a new product idea. To accomplish this selection, it is necessary to screen the many possibilities and reduce the list to a workable number (30 days). Then you must evaluate the remaining ideas and select the one that is unique, that appeals to a large segment of the consumer market, and that is both technologically and economically feasible to produce (60 days).

After the new product has been chosen, you can simultaneously evaluate the possible channels of distribution (10 days), plan both market and technical tests for the product (10 days), and have engineering develop the general specifications of the product (30 days). When you have evaluated the possible channels of distribution, you must evaluate the firm's financial and material resources situation to ensure that all the capital and technical expertise are available (7 days). As soon as you have completed the planning for market and technical tests, you can run a customer survey and begin plans for the extensive marketing required for the introduction of a new product (20 days). After all of the above have been completed, you must obtain top management's approval of the desired plan (1 day).

Once top management's approval is obtained, you can simultaneously select the distribution channel (1 day), set up and produce the pilot run (24 days), develop a marketing program (30 days), and estimate manufacturing costs (4 days). After manufacturing costs are estimated, you can establish a price (5 days). Once you have set up and produced the pilot run and have established the price, you can test market and evaluate the product (60 days). When the test market is complete, the demand forecasts can be made (10 days). You can set up for full production (40 days) after the test market is complete. After determining demand and selecting your distribution channel, you can establish the material suppliers (15 days). When you are set up for full production, material suppliers have been selected, and the market program is complete, you can simultaneously begin production and distribution of your product (30 days) and begin your promotional campaign (30 days). After the promotional campaign and production and distribution are completed, you can release the product for sale (2 days).

Assignment:

1. Draw a project network that depicts the logical sequence of activities required to select and market the new product.
2. What is the critical path?
3. How many days will it take to complete the project?
4. What is the slack for the following activities?
   (a) develop general product specifications
   (b) evaluate distribution channels
   (c) develop marketing program
   (d) set up for full production

3.9. Winter Sports Inc.: In recent years the number of visitors to winter resort areas has been increasing at an exciting rate. The results of an economic feasibility study just completed by members of your staff show that a winter resort complex at the base of Three Finger Jack Butte, which lies in the heart of the Cascade mountain range, could be a profitable venture even with serious energy problems—the area is accessible by car, bus, train, and air. The board of directors have voted to build the five million dollar complex recommended in the study. Unfortunately, due to the short summer season, the complex will have to be built in stages. The first stage (year 1) will contain a day lodge, chair lift, rope tow, generator house (for electricity), and a parking lot designed to accommodate 300 cars and 50 buses. The second and third stages will include a hotel, ice rink, pool, shops, more chair lifts, and other attractions. The board has decided that stage one should begin no later than April 1 and be completed by October 1 in time for the next skiing season. You have been assigned the task of project manager, and it is your job to coordinate the ordering of materials and construction activities to ensure the project's completion by the required date.

After looking into the possible sources of materials, you are confronted with the following time estimates. Materials for the chair lift and rope tow will take 30 days and 12 days, respectively, to arrive once the order is submitted. Lumber for the day lodge, generator hut, and foundations will take 9 days to arrive. The electrical and plumbing materials for the day lodge will take 12 days to arrive. The generator will take 12 days to arrive.

Before actual construction can begin on the various facilities, a road to the site must be built; this will take 6 days. As soon as the road is in, clearing can begin concurrently on the sites of the day lodge, generator house, chair lift, and rope tow. It is estimated that the clearing task at each site will take 6 days, 3 days, 36 days, and 6 days, respectively. The clearing of the main ski slopes can begin after the area for the chair lift has been cleared; this will take 84 days.

The foundation for the day lodge will take 12 days to lay. Construction of the main framework will take an additional 18 days. After the framework is completed, electrical wiring and plumbing can be installed concurrently. These should take 24 and 30 days, respectively. Finally, the finishing construction on the day lodge can begin; this will take 36 days.

Installation of the chair lift towers can begin once the site is cleared, the lumber is delivered, and the foundation is built and poured; all this takes 6 days, and the towers take 67 days. Also, when the chair lift site has been cleared, construction of a permanent road to the upper towers can be started; this will take 24 days. While the towers are being installed, the electric motor to drive the chair lift can be installed; the motor can be installed in 24 days. Once the towers are completed and the motor installed, it will take 3 days to install the cable and an additional 12 days to install the chairs.

Installation of the towers for the rope tow can begin once the site is cleared and the foundation is built and poured; it takes 4 days to build the foundation, pour the concrete and let it cure, and 20 days to install the towers for the rope tow. While the towers are being erected, installation of the electric motor to drive the rope tow can begin; this activity will take 24 days. After the towers and motor are installed, the rope tow can be strung in 1 day. The parking lot can be cleared once the rope tow is finished; this task will take 18 days.

The foundation for the generator house can begin at the same time as the foundation for the lodge; this will take 6 days. The main framework for the generator house can begin once the foundation is completed; framing will take 12 days. After the house is framed the diesel generator can be installed in 18 days. Finishing construction on the generator house can now begin and will take 12 more days.

During the project the workweek will be 6 days. On the basis of the information, draw the project network and answer the following questions:

Assignment:

1. What is the length of the critical path in workdays?
2. Identify the critical path on your network.
3. Can the project be completed by October 1?

PART II
SCHEDULING

Scheduling is the process of converting a plan into an operating timetable. The schedule establishes the start and completion times for all the activities in the project. The original network plan represents a feasible schedule, but the schedule is probably not coordinated and compatible with time constraints imposed on the project and possible resource constraints that may exist. The planning network assumes that the time plan fits any time constraints imposed on the project and that resources are unlimited. This is seldom the case in practice.

Sometimes project due dates, penalty clauses for late completion, and incentives require that the original network plan be expedited. This will require an increase in activity costs. The obvious question is which activities should be allocated the additional resouces to shorten the project duration at minimum cost. Techniques exist for determining a least-cost approach to expediting the project completion time. The next chapter on expediting will be concerned with the *cost-time dimensions* of scheduling.

Labor and equipment levels are usually relatively fixed. Parallel paths often require the same resources simultaneously, a situation which causes excess demands on fixed resource levels. In such situations activities that appear independent on the project network become dependent when the problem of resource allocation is inspected. We will examine two methods which will improve resource scheduling and will deal with *time-resource dimensions*.

Thus, in the next two chapters on scheduling we may find it necessary to relax the assumptions of the time network plan. In other words, in the process of scheduling it may be necessary to adjust start and finish times for activities, extend or expedite the project duration time, and/or exceed the normal level of resources.

4
Low-Cost Scheduling and Expediting

THIS CHAPTER will examine the cost-time dimensions of project scheduling. The end result of the examination will be the development of the total cost curve for the project; its minimum sets the optimum, cost-time schedule. This optimum schedule may differ from the original planning network, the duration set in a contract as a due date, or the duration that results from a resource-constrained schedule. Given the total-cost curve and its minimum point, which is the optimum cost-time schedule, management can compare the cost of meeting any alternative project completion dates with the optimum cost.

THE NEED TO EXPEDITE

In almost every project there is a desire to get the project completed earlier than the date derived from normal activity durations in the original network plan or the optimal cost-time schedule. The problem becomes one of comparing the cost of doing the work more quickly with the optimal cost-time schedule. For example, some contract work specifies awards for the contractor if the project is completed before a particular due date and penalties if the project is completed after the scheduled date. In these cases, it is a simple matter to compare the total project cost for any feasible scheduled date for a contract with the optimum cost-time schedule; the difference represents the cost of meeting the contract date.

Another common situation is the need to release equipment or key people to new projects which are due to start. The cost of cutting project time to release key resources alters the project's total cost. The difference between the optimum cost-time schedule and the new schedule is the cost-time trade-off of releasing the resources at the specific date. Sometimes the reason for expediting simply may be to maintain customer good will. Finally, it is not uncommon to start a project and fall behind schedule midway in the project. The cost of catching up to schedule can be determined easily and quickly. In order to evaluate alternative schedules, we must be able to derive the project total cost curve, which represents the costs for each project duration.

TYPES OF PROJECT COSTS

The total cost for any feasible project duration is the sum of the direct and indirect costs. Both costs vary with time. Figure 4-1 presents an example of the relationship that might be found in a project. The optimum project duration (schedule) is the combination of direct and indirect costs that results in the lowest total cost for the project.

INDIRECT PROJECT COSTS

Indirect costs traditionally are project overhead charges that continue for the life of the project. These costs cannot be associated directly with an individual activity. The bulk of indirect costs is made up of expenses for supervision, general-purpose equipment, administrative staff, interest, taxes, and selling. If bonus or penalty clauses exist in a contract, they usually are included in the indirect cost category, since they apply to the total project rather than to one activity. Usually indirect costs are derived from historical records of costs. Often indirect costs can be expressed as so many dollars per unit of time; hence, with an indirect cost of $100 a day, a project of ten days' duration incurs a total indirect cost of $1,000, whereas a nine-day project duration would incur a total indirect cost of $900—assuming the resources can be used productively if released early. Thus we normally expect indirect costs to decrease if project duration is expedited.

DIRECT PROJECT COSTS

The direct cost for the project is simply the summation of all the individual direct activity costs for the project. The sources of direct costs are direct labor, materials, equipment; direct costs can be tied directly to an activity. Direct costs vary inversely with time; that is, it costs money to buy time off the critical path. Of course, the key is to shorten those individual activities that cost the least to shorten. Note that we reduce critical activities

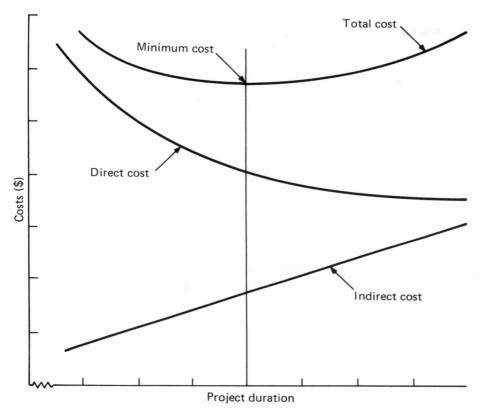

Figure 4-1 Project cost-time relationships

only by compressing project duration. Without a project network plan, the tendency is to expedite all activities in the project to reduce project duration; this is equivalent to a blanket, across-the-board increase in costs, which is indeed a waste.

Recall that in setting activity-time estimates for the project, the network planner assumed that normal operating methods would be used to accomplish the activity. Implicit in "normal operating methods" is the assumption that the task will be performed efficiently and that the method represents the lowest direct cost. Hence, if we wish to shorten project duration by shortening the activity time of an activity on the critical path, it will require more resources (money). For example, if the critical path consisted of only two activities and the costs of expediting the respective activities by one day are $500 and $200, we would select the second activity to compress project duration because it costs the least—$200. Shortening the critical path by one day adds $200 to the total direct cost of the project. This process of shortening an activity duration time is called "crashing" the activity. By computing the least total direct cost for several different feasible project durations, it is possible to derive the curve for the total direct cost of the project shown in Figure 4-1.

DIRECT COST-TIME RELATIONSHIPS

To identify the optimum project cost-time schedule, it is necessary to derive the indirect and direct cost relationships for several different project durations. It is assumed that indirect costs offer little opportunity for varying the level of resources; that is, one more supervisor or secretary will not influence the project completion time. In the process of compressing project duration, indirect costs typically decrease, because the resources are released to other projects, which pick up the overhead burden. Finding the total indirect cost-time points is simply a matter of adding all the indirect costs incurred for different project durations.

Total direct costs of the project are also found by summing all the direct costs of all the individual activities for the project. However, because direct costs for the project increase as project duration is compressed, a systematic method is used to select the individual activities along the critical path(s) that can be expedited at minimum cost. Before demonstrating the selection method, we shall define some new terminology and explain the general approach for selecting activities to be expedited.

NORMAL AND CRASH SITUATIONS

Deriving the total direct-cost curve for a project involves finding the costs of compressing the project duration one time unit at a time. This process requires selecting the individual activity (activities) along the critical path (paths) that can be reduced with the smallest increase in cost per unit of time. The basis for activity selection is identification of the normal and crash times and the direct costs associated with each time point. *Normal time* is the activity time given in the original project network; normal assumes the use of normal and efficient methods. *Normal cost* is the direct cost of the activity associated with completing the activity in normal time. *Crash time* is the minimum time possible to complete the activity, if no reasonable costs are spared to reduce the activity duration; it represents a time limit in which the use of additional resources will not reduce activity time. *Crash cost* is the activity direct cost required to complete the activity in the minimum possible time.

An example of normal and crash situations is a road construction crew filling dirt into a large canyon. Under normal conditions three tractors, working a single shift five days a week, would be used for twelve weeks to complete the fill. The normal cost would be $75,000. Management concludes that the fill activity can be crashed to a minimum of six weeks, using eight tractors during the daylight hours. The crash cost for the fill activity would be $200,000. Note that crashing decreases the efficiency of resources (increases cost), since the normal time is efficient by definition.

Figure 4-2 is a hypothetical activity cost-time trade-off graph. The vertical axis represents the activity's direct cost; the horizontal axis represents activity duration. The normal and crash time-cost points are connected with a straight line, which assumes that the cost-time relationship is linear; that is, the cost of buying one unit of activity time is constant within the normal and crash time interval. If the slope of the line is relatively flat, the cost of expediting is small; conversely, as the slope steepens, the cost of expediting increases. Again, observe that the normal and crash situations represent constraints of cost and time, and all expediting must occur within the normal and crash interval.

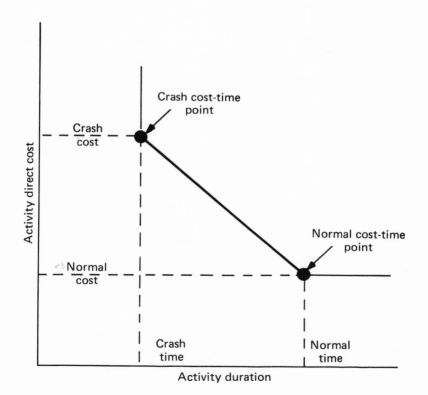

Figure 4-2 Activity cost-time trade-off graph

The assumption of the linear relationship between cost and time within the normal and crash interval is open to question. Actually, the relationship may take a variety of forms; however, the original cost-time trade-off procedures assume linearity on the basis of its simplicity, and that linearity represents a reasonable approximation of the relationship for scheduling purposes. (Nonlinearity is discussed below in this chapter.)

COST SLOPE

The objective of compressing the project schedule is to reduce those activities on the critical path(s) that cost the least to shorten. The method for selecting the activity to reduce is to compare the cost slopes of all eligible activities. *Cost slope* is the incremental cost of reducing the activity duration time. The equation is as follows:

$$\text{cost slope} = \frac{\text{crash cost} - \text{normal cost}}{\text{normal time} - \text{crash time}}$$

or symbolically

$$CS = \frac{CC - NC}{NT - CT}$$

(Because compression requires moving from normal toward crash time, the terms in the denominator are reversed to make the slope positive.)

Let us use this equation in an example. Assume that the normal activity time and cost are seven days and $500, and that the crash time and cost are five days and $900. The cost slope is computed as follows:

$$CS = \frac{CC - NC}{NT - CT} = \frac{\$900 - \$500}{7 - 5} = \frac{\$400}{2} = \$200 \text{ per day}$$

By selecting and reducing the activity duration of the activity or activities with the smallest slope, the additional total direct cost of compression is minimized. This method is used to compress the project completion time and to determine the total direct costs for alternative project durations. The concept of cost slope is very important in understanding the cost-time trade-off procedure.

COST-TIME TRADE-OFF PROCEDURE

The procedure for finding the project duration that will minimize total cost is straightforward and easy to compute for small networks. The cost-time procedure provides a method for finding the *total* cost curve for the project. The lowest point on the total cost curve is the optimum cost-time scheduled date. Given the optimum schedule, it is possible to compare any alternative scheduled completion date to find the additional cost. The total cost curve represents total project costs over a range of project durations. For any selected duration, the total cost is the sum of the total direct plus total indirect costs for the project. Thus, if we have the direct and indirect costs for each duration, we can plot the three curves—direct, indirect, and total cost. The most difficult curve to find is the direct cost curve; the procedure that follows provides a method for deriving this curve. When the direct costs are added to the indirect, the total cost curve is derived and the optimum cost-time schedule found.

The cost-time trade-off procedure includes seven steps. These steps will be clarified by working through the following example:

Step 1. Collect normal and crash times and costs for all activities in the project planning network. A hypothetical project network is shown in Figure 4-3. Table 4-1 presents the normal and crash times and costs for each activity in the network.

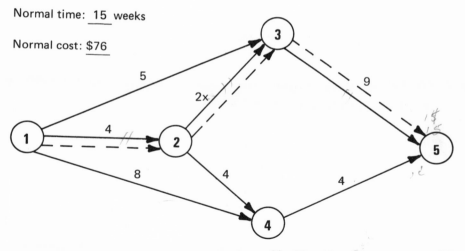

Normal time: 15 weeks

Normal cost: $76

x = Maximum improvement reached

Figure 4-3 Cost-time trade-off network: 15 weeks

TABLE 4-1. NORMAL AND CRASH COSTS.
(thousands of dollars)

Activity	Normal Time (Weeks)	Normal Direct Cost	Crash Time	Crash Direct Cost	Cost Slope (Expediting Cost Per Unit Of Time)	Maximum Improvement	Time Units Crashed
1-2	4	$ 5	3	$12	$ 7	1	
1-3	5	9	3	19	5	2	
1-4	8	11	5	41	10	3	
2-3	2	20	2	20	0	0	
2-4	4	8	3	18	10	1	
3-5	9	14	5	58	11	4	
4-5	4	9	3	18	9	1	

Total Direct Cost $76

Step 2. Compute the total direct costs at normal time. This figure is computed by summing all the direct normal costs of all the activities in the project. In this example, the total direct cost at normal is $76 (5+9+11 +20+8+14+9). This amount represents the first point (lowest) on the total direct cost curve.

Step 3. Compute the cost slope for each activity and find the maximum units of time each activity can be crashed. The cost slope represents the cost to buy one unit of time off an activity duration. Table 4-1 shows the cost slope or expediting cost per unit of time and the maximum improvement possible for each activity in the network. The slope or expediting cost per unit of time is computed by using the equation explained in the preceding section. For example, the slope of activity 1-3 is $5 per week $(19-9)/(5-3)$, and the maximum improvement possible is 2 weeks $(5-3)$— the difference between the normal and crash times.

Step 4. Construct a total direct cost curve over a range of project durations—or until reduction of critical activities is impossible. In this example, let us determine the direct cost points from the normal project duration of 15 weeks to a crashed duration of 10 weeks.

15-week schedule: The first point is the 15-week schedule. The total direct costs were determined to be $76 (from Step 2); this schedule and its costs are shown in Figure 4-3.

14-week schedule: When there is only one critical path in the network, simply reduce the low-cost critical activity to gain one time unit. In the example network the critical path is 1,2,3,5. Activity 1–2 costs $7 to reduce; activity 2–3 cannot be reduced; and activity 3–5 costs $11 to reduce. Because activity 1–2 costs the least to reduce, we will reduce this activity one time unit at an additional cost of $7. See Figure 4-4. This change reduces the project duration to 14 weeks and increases the total direct costs from $76 to $83 (76+7). Expediting the project from 15 to 14 weeks creates two critical paths (1,2,3,5 and 1,3,5). Note that activity 1–2 has been crashed as much as possible.

13-week schedule: If more than one critical path exists, the trick is to find the single activity or combination of activities that will shorten all critical paths at the least cost. In the example, activity 3–5 is common to both critical paths. Since neither activity 1–2 nor 2–3 can be shortened— activity 2–3 cannot be crashed, and activity 1–2 has been crashed to its maximum improvement—the only choice is to shorten activity 3–5 to 7 weeks, increase the total direct costs to $94 (83+11), and reduce the project duration to 13 weeks. See Figure 4-5.

14-week schedule

Total direct cost: 76 + 7 = 83

Activity changed: 1-2 Cost: $7

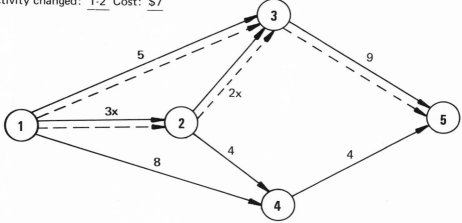

Figure 4-4   Cost-time trade-off network: 14 weeks

13-week schedule

Total direct cost: 83 + 11 = 94

Activity changed: 3-5   Cost: $11

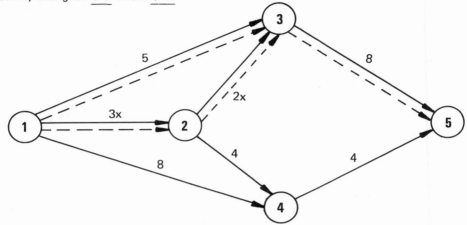

Figure 4-5   Cost-time trade-off network: 13 weeks

12-week schedule: A schedule of 12 weeks requires that activity 3–5 be shortened again. Figure 4-6 shows this change; the total direct cost is now $105 (94+11). Note that there are now three critical paths—1,3,5; 1,2,3,5; and 1–4–5.

11-week schedule: When we reach a situation where several parallel critical paths exist, it is usually necessary to test every combination of activities that can reduce the project duration to find the low-cost combination. In large networks this is a tedious chore that can be handled best by a computer; however, in the simple project network here the tedium is limited. Activities 3–5, 1–4, and 4–5 are eligible for reduction. Note that activity 1–3 is excluded, because, to reduce it one time unit would not reduce the project duration, since activities 1–2 and 2–3 have been crashed as much as possible. Activity 3–5 can be reduced with 1–4 or 4–5 to shorten the project duration. The cost of expediting activities 3–5 and 1–4 one week is $21 (11+10); the cost for 3–5 and 4–5 is $20 (11+9). The low-cost combination is 3–5 and 4–5 for a $20 increase in direct cost to expedite one time unit. See Figure 4-7. Observe that the total direct cost is now $125.

10-week schedule: A 10-week schedule can be attained only by reducing activities 1–4 and 3–5 at a cost of $21 (10+11). The total direct cost for

12-week schedule

Total direct cost: 94 + 11 = 105

Activity changed: 3-5 Cost: $11

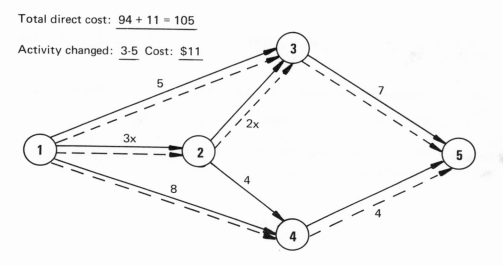
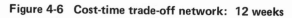

Figure 4-6 Cost-time trade-off network: 12 weeks

11-week schedule
Total direct cost: 105 + 11 + 9 = 125

	Activities changed	Cost
	3-5	$11
	4-5	$ 9

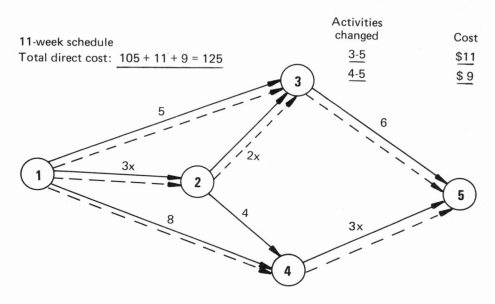

Figure 4-7 Cost-time trade-off network: 11 weeks

a project duration of 10 weeks is $146 (125+21). See Figure 4-8. We have now identified enough direct cost-duration points to test for a low-cost schedule.

Step 5. Collect the total indirect costs over the same range of project durations. Those responsible for accounting would be the best source for the indirect or overhead costs that will accompany a given project. Normally, these costs can be expected to decrease as the project duration is decreased.

Step 6. Compute the optimum cost-time schedule. The optimum cost-time schedule is found by summing the total direct and indirect costs for each project duration and then selecting the project duration with the lowest total costs for the project. Figure 4-9 exhibits the total direct costs computed in Step 4, the total indirect costs provided by accounting, and the total costs for each duration. From the table it is obvious that the lowest cost project schedule is 13 weeks. The same cost relationships are shown graphically below the table. Observe that the low-cost schedule of 13 weeks is less than the original planning network, which had a project duration of 15 weeks. When overhead costs are significant, almost always the optimum cost-time schedule will be less than the project duration found in the planning network. In fact, as long as the indirect savings are greater than the increase in direct costs, the optimum cost-time schedule will be less than the planning network duration.

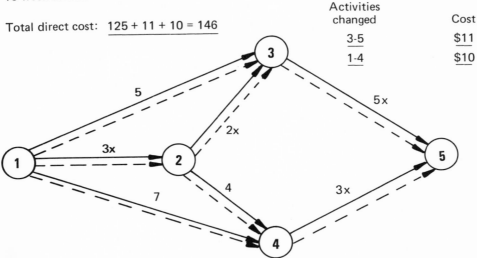

10-week schedule

Total direct cost: 125 + 11 + 10 = 146

Activities changed	Cost
3-5	$11
1-4	$10

Figure 4-8 Cost-time trade-off network: 10 weeks

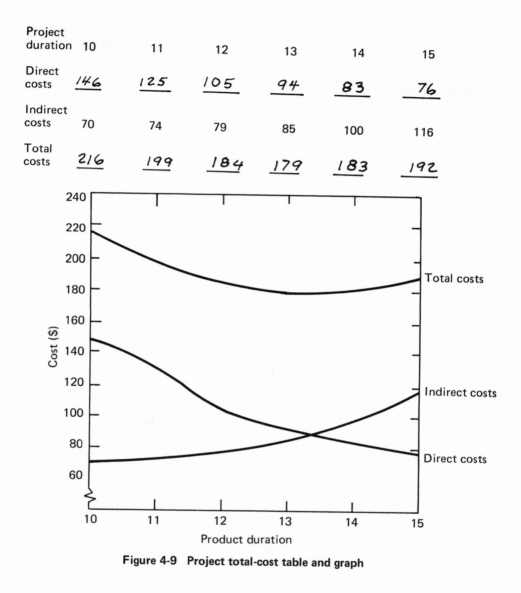

Project duration	10	11	12	13	14	15
Direct costs	146	125	105	94	83	76
Indirect costs	70	74	79	85	100	116
Total costs	216	199	184	179	183	192

Figure 4-9   Project total-cost table and graph

Step 7. Compare the optimum cost-time schedule with any alternative schedule that may be under consideration. Often there are compelling reasons for delaying the completion of a project—or the reverse of completing the project by a specific date. For example, if a key piece of equipment is not available for a critical activity on its scheduled day, the project may have to be delayed until the equipment becomes available. The difference between the optimum project duration cost and the cost at the delayed date represents the cost-time trade-off of not having the equipment available. With this cost in mind, the manager can easily consider other alternatives that may be available.

Another situation that is common in construction and research and development is the incentive contract. In the hypothetical example, add the following condition: If there is a bonus (savings) is $6 for each week the project is completed before 15 weeks, when would the manager prefer to complete the project? Table 4-2 shows that the 12-week schedule is now the low-cost schedule (rather than the 13-week), when the incentive is included in the analysis. The opposite of the incentive—a penalty—also is common in construction; penalties are handled in the same manner except that the penalty is *added* to costs. The total cost curve is useful to contractors in contract negotiation, and is useful midway in the project when the project is behind schedule and it is necessary to catch up.

TABLE 4-2. LOW-COST SCHEDULE WITH INCENTIVE.

Project Duration	10	11	12	13	14	15
Total Cost	$216	199	184	179	183	192
Less Incentive Saving	$ 30	24	18	12	6	0
Resultant Cost	$186	175	(166)	167	177	192

ASSUMPTIONS OF COST-TIME TRADE-OFF PROCEDURE

Usually, attempts to make routine the decision-making process with a set of rules necessitates having to live with a set of assumptions that allow the rules to be useful. The cost-time trade-off procedure is no exception and should be used with a clear understanding of the assumptions which underlie it. The key assumptions the manager should be aware of are these:

1. The method assumes resources are unlimited and available.

2. The normal time for the activity represents the low-cost and efficient method.

3. The relationship between time and cost is linear.

If resources are not available for the date they are scheduled, we may be directing attention to the wrong problem. The problem may be one requiring attention to managing limited resources rather than concentrating on cost. Chapter 5 deals with scheduling scarce resources.

The second assumption makes good practical sense, in that the normal mode of operation should be efficient and low cost. This assumption is necessary because the cost-time procedure requires that the cost-time relationship is an increasing one as time is compressed.

The third assumption of linearity has received a great deal of attention in the literature because it is believed that the cost-time relationship may be nonlinear. The section that follows discusses the assumption and possible modifications that can be made to accommodate nonlinearity.

Nonlinearity

It is impossible to generalize concerning the cost-time relationship because it depends on the nature of the activity. Figure 4-10 contains four nonlinear relationships. The curve in part (a) presents a common cost-time relationship found in practice. This convex relationship assumes that the initial reductions cost less than those near the crash situation. The notion behind this relationship is that as resources are added to compress activity duration, the efficiency of each additional unit of the resource decreases. Thus the costs of compressing activity time when the relationship is convex increases at an increasing rate as the crash point is approached.

The curve in part (b) depicts the opposite relationship (concave) of part (a). Here the initial units of resources added are more expensive relative to those added near the crash situation. Although this cost-time relationship is not as common as the convex relationship, situations do exist where the curve closely approximates the true relationship.

If the actual cost-time relationship is similar to those depicted in parts (a) and (b), and the linear relationship would result in significant errors, a piecewise linear "curve" can be used to approximate the true curve. By cutting the curve into segments and assigning a linear relationship for each segment, a reasonably close fit can be made to the true cost-time curve. Part (c) shows a piecewise cost curve with multiple crash points—C_1, C_2, C_3.

A possible explanation of the piecewise linear curve is as follows: the normal cost-time point (N) represents regular work time and cost. The linear segment N-C_1 represents time reduced by overtime work. The linear segment C_1-C_2 represents overtime and weekend work. The final segment, C_2-C_3, represents an increase in the size or level of the crew being used. Note that since this curve is convex, the slope of each successive linear seg-

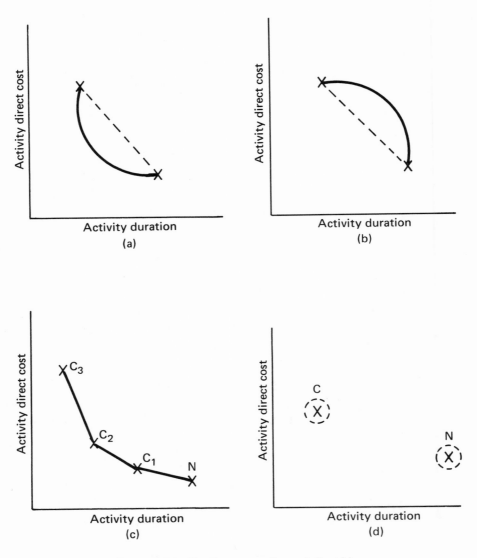

Figure 4-10 Nonlinear cost-time relationships

ment increases as you move away from the normal situation to the crash point. By using piecewise linear approximations with multiple crash points, it is possible to approximate the shape of any continuous curve (for example, an S curve). A closer approximation of the curve can be made by increasing the number of segments.

Part (d) presents two discrete points for the normal and crash situations; the continuous, linear relationship does not exist. Fixed points can occur when different contractors or subcontractors bid to perform an activity. The result may be that each firm will submit a different finish time and cost. One contractor submits the time and cost labeled "N," while another contractor submits the time and cost labeled "C." Fixed-point relationships also can occur when different methods are used to perform the task; for example, a ripe mountainous timber stand can be clear-cut using either crawler tractors or a high line that carries the logs to a truck landing.

Defense of the Linearity Assumption

As nonlinear curves can be approximated with piecewise linear segments, it is possible to maintain the linearity assumption. Piecewise linear curves and discrete normal and crash points will not make significant changes in the original cost-time trade-off methods used by Kelly and Walker.* They based their rationale for the linearity assumption between normal and crash points on several practical factors. First, and most important, by assuming linearity, the computational method of making successive time reductions on the critical path is greatly simplified. Second, there is no a priori evidence that any nonlinear function would be a better approximation of the true cost-time relationship. Third, gathering the actual direct costs for different activity durations would be a difficult task even if such data were available. Finally, because of the uncertainty of cost and time estimates and the on-going changes that occur after the project is started, linear approximations, although rough, can be used to develop quickly a low-cost schedule that is very likely near the optimum. These factors have led to the almost exclusive use of linear mathematical algorithms for compressing project completion times.

CONCLUSIONS

Cost-time trade-off procedures allow the project manager to place a dollar value on change. Figure 4-11 presents a flowchart of the procedure presented in this chapter. The method usually gives an optimal or near-optimal answer. There is a rare set of conditions that can occur as the project is compressed more and more and additional critical paths are created. Sometimes in the process of compressing the project schedule, a path that is critical and has been compressed will become noncritical. When this happens,

---

* Kelly, J. E., "Critical Path Planning and Scheduling: Mathematical Basis," in *Operations Research*, vol. 9, no. 3 (1961) pp. 296-320.

it is possible to "uncrash" or buy back the time of an activity that was previously compressed and thus avoid the cost of expediting the activity. Since these conditions are not common in practice, the buy-back feature was omitted from the main text of the chapter; instead, the interested student will find this feature discussed in the appendix to this chapter.

In practice the cost of collecting the information needed for the cost-time trade-off method and the accuracy of the cost estimates has been questioned. The cost of collecting the information has not been found to be large where the costs of the project are important and the potential savings significant. Others question the accuracy of the cost estimates and conclude that the procedure is not useful. If knowing the dollar value of a proposed change is important—as it usually is in project management—the argument about accuracy is held in a leaky bucket. More important, what is the alternative to not making cost estimates to evaluate proposed changes in the project duration? Rough normal and crash cost estimates give the manager a chance to evaluate the relative cost of change and to make an educated decision; the complete avoidance of cost estimates may not be much better than flipping a coin.

The methods discussed in this chapter can be done informally, manually, or with a computer. The usefulness of the informal method is limited by the experience and capacity of the manager to remember costs; hence, this method is most effective in small projects. Manual computation of the cost-time trade-off procedure becomes very tedious and a difficult search procedure as the number of parallel and connecting paths increase; consequently, this usually restricts manual methods to small projects. For projects of formidable size, every major computer company has computer programs available that will perform the procedures suggested in this chapter.

APPENDIX

The cost-time trade-off procedure given in the flowchart in Figure 4-11 is adequate for most networks; however, under certain circumstances buying back time or "uncrashing" may be possible. The network in Figure 4-12a can be used to illustrate the special set of circumstances which allows the buying back of time. The critical path is 1,2,3,5, and the project duration is 11 weeks. Part (b) shows the project compressed to a 9-week schedule by using the regular cost-time procedures. Assuming all activities can be compressed, the next move to compress the project duration to 8 weeks requires that activities 1–2 and 3–5 be reduced simultaneously. Note that shortening these activities results in path 1,2,3,5 being shortened 2 weeks, and the path is no longer critical. Consequently, it is possible to buy back one week (add a week) from activity 2–3 and save $10; path 1,2,3,5 is

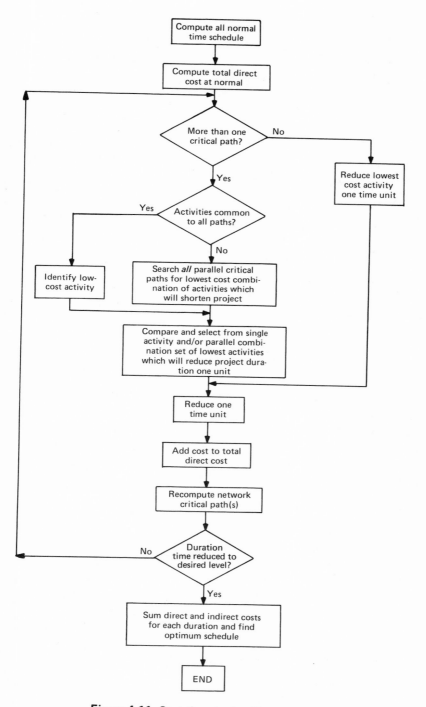

Figure 4-11 Cost-time trade-off network

again critical. The direct cost for reducing the project from 9 weeks to 8 weeks is $50 (40+20−10). Part (c) shows the final reduction. Of course, if more than one activity connects the two critical paths, the activity that is the most expensive should be chosen as the first activity to be "un-crashed," or to buy back time from.

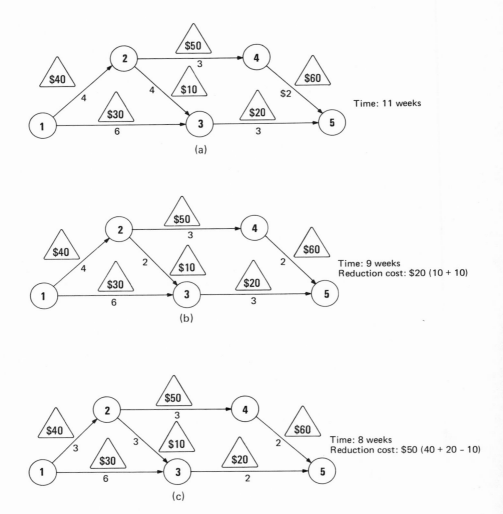

Figure 4-12   Buy-back procedure

In short, anytime two or more critical paths are connected, and the connecting activities have been compressed already, there is the potential that a buy-back situation can occur. The signal to watch for during the normal cost-time trade-off procedure is one in which compression of the project duration results in a critical path switching to one that is not critical. If a computer is used, the programs provided by the computer companies usually have the buy-back feature included in them.

QUESTIONS

4-1. What are the assumptions of cost-time trade-off procedures?

4-2. How do cost-time trade-off procedures avoid across-the-board increases in cost when the project must be compressed?

4-3. Why does the assumption of a linear relationship between cost and time not limit the value or use of cost-time procedures?

4-4. What costs might normally be included in indirect project cost?

4-5. Under what conditions would you expect a buy-back situation to occur?

4-6. If the original plan of a project has time estimates that are presently low-cost and efficient methods, how is it possible that the optimum cost-time schedule usually has a project duration that is less than the duration found in the plan?

EXERCISES

4-1.

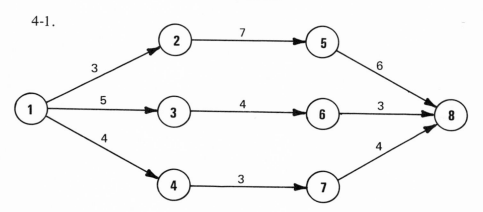

A project network is given above. Below, normal and crash times and costs are given for each activity in the project along with incremental costs (slope) and the maximum time improvement possible for the activity.

ACTIVITY ID	NORMAL TIME	NORMAL COST	CRASH TIME	CRASH COST	INCREM. COST	MAX. IMPROVE.
1-2	3	$ 50	2	$110	$60	1
1-3	5	100	4	150	50	1
1-4	4	80	4	80	0	0
2-5	7	40	5	100	30	2
3-6	4	80	4	80	0	0
4-7	3	200	3	200	0	0
5-8	6	70	4	150	40	2
6-8	3	40	3	40	0	0
7-8	4	60	3	130	70	1
		$720				

The indirect costs for each project duration are $700 for 16 weeks, 600 for 15, 500 for 14, 400 for 13, 300 for 12, and 200 for 11 weeks. Use the procedure developed in this chapter (one period at a time) to find the total costs for each duration.

What is the optimum cost-time schedule? Is it different from the project duration developed in the plan? Plot the direct, indirect, and total costs on a graph.

4-2. The normal and crash times and direct costs for a project are given below. The indirect costs for selected durations are also given. Using the procedures of this chapter, develop the direct and total costs for each duration listed.

ACTIVITY ID	NORMAL TIME	NORMAL COST	CRASH TIME	CRASH COST	PROJECT DURATION	INDIRECT COST
1-2	8	$ 40	6	$120	19	$200
1-3	6	60	5	90	18	180
1-4	5	30	4	50	17	160
2-3	7	20	5	40	16	140
2-5	10	10	7	70	15	120
4-5	12	50	11	100		
3-5	4	0	4	0		
		$210				

4-3. Information for a cost-time trade-off problem is given below. Compute the direct, indirect, and total costs for each project duration. Plot each of these costs on a graph. What is the optimum cost-time schedule?

ACTIVITY ID	NORMAL TIME	NORMAL COST	CRASH TIME	CRASH COST	PROJECT DURATION	INDIRECT COST
1-2	7	$ 60	5	200	16	$1200
1-3	4	30	3	40	15	1130
2-4	4	40	2	80	14	1000
2-5	5	110	2	260	13	900
3-6	1	80	1	80	12	860
4-7	2	60	1	90	11	820
5-7	2	70	1	110	10	790
6-7	5	90	2	690		
7-8	2	140	2	140		

4-4. From the information given below for a cost-time trade-off problem, compute the direct, indirect, and total costs for each project duration. What is the optimum cost-time schedule? The customer offers you $10 for every week you can cut from the normal time on your original planning network. Would you take it? If so, for how many weeks? Why?

ACTIVITY ID	NORMAL TIME	NORMAL COST	CRASH TIME	CRASH COST	PROJECT DURATION	INDIRECT COST
1-2	10	$ 40	8	$200	27	$300
1-3	5	80	4	120	26	240
1-4	8	10	5	100	25	180
2-4	11	50	9	150	24	120
3-4	15	100	11	500	23	60
4-5	6	20	5	50	22	50

4-5. The project manager gives you the network information below. For each week you analyze, show the total direct costs, critical path(s), and activity(ies) changed to decrease the project duration one week.

ACTIVITY ID	NORMAL TIME	NORMAL COST	CRASH TIME	CRASH COST	PROJECT DURATION	INDIRECT COST
1-2	3	$ 50	2	$140	15	$1250
1-3	6	110	1	360	14	1100
1-4	7	135	4	735	13	755
2-3	2	70	1	155	12	500
2-6	4	80	4	80	11	350
3-5	5	85	2	535	10	225
4-5	3	60	2	170		
4-7	6	75	4	375		
5-7	4	40	2	180		
6-7	4	95	4	95		

4-6. The normal and crash times and costs for a project are given below. Find the total direct, indirect, and total costs for each project duration. List the activities changed to reduce the project duration one time unit (for each duration). What is the optimum cost-time schedule?

ACTIVITY ID	NORMAL TIME	NORMAL COST	CRASH TIME	CRASH COST	PROJECT DURATION	INDIRECT COST
1-2	8	$ 60	7	$120	19	$700
1-4	9	100	6	160	18	600
1-5	4	40	3	50	17	500
2-3	3	40	1	180	16	400
2-4	4	100	2	500	15	300
3-6	6	80	5	100	14	200
4-6	4	50	2	150		
4-7	2	10	1	30		
4-8	4	30	2	50		
5-7	7	20	5	40		
6-8	2	10	1	40		
7-8	4	50	3	100		

4-7. The normal and crash times and costs are given below. Compute the total direct cost and total cost for each project duration. When would you prefer to see the project completed?

ACTIVITY ID	NORMAL TIME	NORMAL COST	CRASH TIME	CRASH COST	PROJECT DURATION	INDIRECT COST
1-2	8	$30	7	$ 70	30	$210
			6	270	29	150
1-3	15	10	15	10	28	120
1-4	5	10	5	10	27	80
2-4	12	60	11	120	26	40
			9	360		
3-4	4	20	3	100		
			2	240		
4-5	10	40	9	120		

4-8. Compute the total direct cost and total cost for each project duration, given the information below. What is the optimum schedule?

ACTIVITY ID	NORMAL TIME	NORMAL COST	CRASH TIME	CRASH COST	PROJECT DURATION	INDIRECT COST
1-2	5	$5	4	$12	14	$25
1-4	10	3	10	3	13	20
2-3	6	4	5	8	12	15
2-4	6	5	4	9	11	10
2-5	5	8	3	16		
3-5	3	6	2	9		
4-5	2	5	1	10		

4-9. Twelve-Meter Yacht Construction (A): Sailcup Corporation is a syndicated group of yachtsmen planning the construction of a twelve-meter yacht for the America's Cup Trial races to be held in June of the coming year.

The yacht needs to be completed on or before the twenty-fifth week to ensure at least a small amount of sailing time in San Diego before it is transported to Newport, R.I., where the trial races are held. You have been assigned the task of project manager, and it is your job to coordinate the ordering of materials and construction activities to ensure completion of the project by the required date.

Before construction can begin, the naval architect who has been doing the design work must formalize his ideas and make the blueprints for the hull, deck, mast, and fittings; this will take 2 weeks.

As soon as the blueprints are done, the boat builders can start building the aluminum hull; the hull will take 8 weeks to complete. At the same time, the deck fittings and mast can be ordered; delivery will be in 11 and 8 weeks, respectively. The deck for the yacht cannot be started until the hull is completed. The deck will take an additional 6 weeks; then the fittings can be installed. The fittings require 7 weeks to complete.

Through some clever planning, painting with epoxy-graphite can begin as soon as construction of the hull ends; painting requires 4 weeks to do the job properly.

As soon as the mast has been fabricated, it can be shipped to the sail-maker, who will test the mast for deflections and then construct the sails. About 20 sails must be made—a process that will take 9 weeks, including transport back to the boatyard.

Once all the pieces are together and the hull is painted, it will take 1 week to step (put in place) the mast and do the touch-up work on the deck.

Assignment:

    a. What is the length of the critical path? Identify it on your network.

    b. Can the job be done by the twenty-fifth week?

Twelve-Meter Yacht Construction (B): The skipper of the yacht, Jim Oarsman, sent a letter to the syndicate head saying that if the yacht is not done 7 weeks earlier than shown on the project network, so he can have more time to sail it in San Diego Bay, he will quit as the helmsman for the yacht. The syndicate head has called you and asked if the $100,000 available for such an emergency will cover the added costs of production needed to get the job done 7 weeks earlier than planned.

Use the figures below in addition to your network from (A) to calculate the additional money needed. Make a decision as to whether Jim Oarsman can be retained as helmsman, considering the information available to you.

ACTIVITY ID	NORMAL TIME	NORMAL COST	CRASH TIME	CRASH COST
design	2	10,000	1	18,000
hull	8	50,000	5	140,000
O. mast	8	25,000	4	29,000
O. deck fit	11	45,000	8	75,000
deck	6	4,000	4	9,000
paint	4	18,000	3	27,000
sails	9	7,000	3	19,000
inst. fit	7	15,000	5	33,000
step	1	9,000	1	9,000

5
Resource Scheduling

THE RESOURCE utilization problem is one of the most important problems which the project manager must face. Network planning will not be helpful if the resources—labor and equipment—are not available at the right time and place and in the correct quantities. The potential savings or losses which can occur because of efficient or inefficient scheduling of resouces are large and deserve management's attention.

A resource schedule which establishes start and finish times for each project resource is necessary to forecast resource needs for the duration of the project. This same resource schedule is also used to facilitate control as the project nears completion. Many large cost overruns of contractors can be tied to a lack of realistic resource schedules.

This chapter first identifies the types of scheduling problems encountered in practice. Next, it discusses in detail the methods used to schedule time- and resource-constrained projects, and then looks at some extensions of the simplified methods of scheduling. Finally, it will be shown that all of the principles which apply to single projects also apply to multiprojects and multiresource projects.

TYPES OF SCHEDULING PROBLEMS

When resources are to be scheduled, the project manager must decide whether the project is *time constrained* or *resource constrained*. If time is fixed, resources must be flexible; if resources are fixed, project duration must be flexible. Any scheduling routine available today requires that the project be identified as time constrained or resource constrained. This is very difficult to do in practice, but the project must be one or the other (even if it is decided quality will be sacrificed).

TIME-CONSTRAINED PROJECTS

Time-constrained projects have a set deadline for the completion of the project. Frequently, the assurance of getting the project completed by a specific date is of key importance to those concerned. In fact, construction contracts are sometimes awarded because of a contractor's ability to get the project completed by the contract due date. Incentives and/or penalties are not uncommon in construction projects. If the project is completed before the contract due date, the contractor is awarded an incentive for each day of early completion. Conversely, if the project is finished late, the contractor pays a penalty for each day late. For example, construction of the U.S. pavillion at the 1964 World's Fair included incentives and penalties as did a few of the contracts for moon exploration. Road contracts often include penalty clauses.

In time-constrained projects it is assumed that resouces are unlimited. In a practical sense this means the resources needed will be purchased or made available—often at additional cost. The main concern is to keep the resource pool as small as possible and still get the project completed by the due date.

RESOURCE-CONSTRAINED PROBLEMS

In practice most firms have relatively fixed levels of work force and equipment. The ability of a firm to take on a new project often depends to a large extent on the availability of resources from a relatively fixed resource pool. Even if resources (such as labor) are assembled specifically for the project, they are usually committed for the duration of the project. The problem is to schedule project activities so the resources available in the pool are not exceeded and the original network relationships are not violated. The effect of a limited resource pool is that often activities which appear to be independent and parallel on the network may be dependent and sequential in the schedule. This forced sequential scheduling results in a reduction in the amount of slack for replanning and rescheduling. For example, an earth-moving construction company may be limited by its equipment of three bulldozers, six trucks, and one grader; if two parallel activities call for the three bulldozers simultaneously and slack is minimal, it will be necessary to schedule the activities sequentially, a move which may use up the existing slack and possibly extend the project duration. Scheduling within the limits of the resource pool enhances better utilization of available resources and avoids the costs of adding to the resource pool, but it also implies that the project duration can be slipped if resources are not adequate.

HYPOTHETICAL EXAMPLES

Two simple examples of time-constrained and resource-constrained projects will aid in understanding the basic nature of the resource scheduling problems the project manager may experience in practice.

A TIME-CONSTRAINED SCHEDULING PROBLEM

In time-constrained projects it is assumed the project must be completed on time and resources will be made available. The scheduling problem for these projects is one of *reducing the peak level of resources required and reducing the fluctuations in the demand for the resource.* The standard PERT/CPM network usually produces an uneven resource profile over the duration of the project. Generally (if an early start schedule is assumed), demand for the resource will build up to a peak and then taper off. Since the resource pool must be large enough to cover the peak demand for the resource, savings accrue if the peak can be reduced. Further, savings result from *smoothing* or *leveling* the resource profile, thereby reducing variation in demand for a resource. For example, hiring and layoff costs or equipment setup costs can be avoided if the resource level is constant. A constant level of labor utilization avoids idle time costs, increased unemployment, poor morale, poor community relations, and decreased productivity. Equipment costs behave in a similar manner; that is, meeting fluctuations in demand for equipment usually means additional moving costs, setup costs, higher renting costs, and in many cases more idle equipment time. Thus, sharp resource fluctuations should be minimized. Resource fluctuations can be minimized even if resource availability is assumed "unlimited" by using existing slack time to smooth the peaks and valleys of the resource demanded.

The hypothetical example in Figure 5-1 illustrates a time-constrained project. Assume the only resource is labor and only one skill is involved. Assume further that the project duration of eight weeks shown in the time network plan is the critical date on which the project must be completed. The number of workers required for each activity is shown in parentheses on the activity arrows in the network. As a starting point, an early start schedule is created to show the nature of the labor pool required if each activity is started on its earliest expected time. Part (a) presents the schedule in bar chart form. Although this early start schedule is feasible, it is not practical. Early start schedules tend to push resource requirements to the left on the time scale and cause excessive demands early in the project; this results in labor requirements that are not level and that include fluctuations of significant magnitude. The plotted histogram of the total number of workers required for each period depicts the results of the early start schedule more clearly. The first three weeks require three workers; the fourth requires four; the fifth, two; and one for the remainder of the project.

Given the amount of slack in the network, a smoother work schedule seems possible. Figure 5-1b presents a feasible schedule developed by trial-and-error reshuffling of the activity start times using slack times of noncritical activities. The solution does not violate the original network sequence or times, and the solution meets the eight-week deadline. A steady work force of two people can be used for the duration of the project; the fluctuations have been reduced to having one additional worker available during the third and eighth weeks.

A RESOURCE-CONSTRAINED SCHEDULING PROBLEM

Resource-constrained projects are more common than time-constrained ones. Although it is possible to add resources at additional cost, most project managers must schedule within relatively fixed resource pools, for example, labor and equipment pools. If the resource pool is relatively "tight" or restrictive, the possibility of extending the project completion date increases. Fixed resource constraints usually cause some resources to be scheduled serially, rather than in parallel, thereby reducing available slack.

In resource-constrained problems the scheduling objective is to minimize project duration without exceeding the resource limit. Figure 5-2 presents the same network and resource requirements given in Figure 5-1. The only difference is that instead of the duration time being fixed, the labor resource pool is limited to two workers. Using trial-and-error methods it is possible to find the optimal solution given in the bar chart schedule. Although the total requirements for any given week do not exceed the two-worker fixed resource limit, the project duration has been extended to nine weeks because of the fixed resource limit. Observe that the critical path and slack are no longer relevant; in order to meet the two-worker constraint the activities must be performed as scheduled.

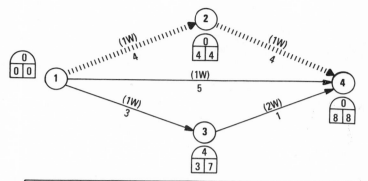

Network Information						Resource Loading Chart								
Act. No.	Dur.	No work-ers	ES	LF	Slack	Week Number								
						1	2	3	4	5	6	7	8	
1-2	4	1	0	4	0	[/	/	/	/]					
1-4	5	1	0	8	3	[/	/	/	/	/			]	
1-3	3	1	0	7	4	[/	/	/				]		
2-4	4	1	4	8	0				[/	/	/	/]		
3-4	1	2	3	8	4			[2					]	
ES Labor Requirements						3	3	3	4	2	/	/	/	

Early start schedule

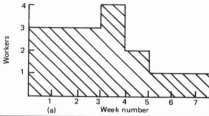

Histogram of early start labor requirements

Network Information						Resource Loading Chart								
Act. No.	Dur.	No. Work-ers	ES	LF	Slack	Week Number								
						1	2	3	4	5	6	7	8	
1-2	4	1	0	4	0	[/	/	/	/]					
1-4	5	1	0	8	3	[		/	/	/	/	/	]	
1-3	3	1	0	7	4	[/	/	/				]		
2-4	4	1	4	8	0				[/	/	/	/]		
3-4	1	2	3	8	4				[				2]	
Leveled Labor Requirements						2	2	3	2	2	2	2	3	

Leveled schedule fixed project duration (8 weeks)

Histogram of smoothed labor for 8-week schedule

(b)

Figure 5-1 Time-constrained project

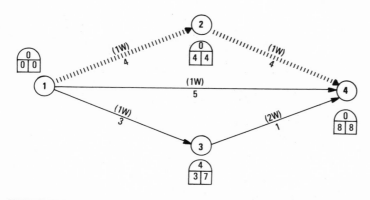

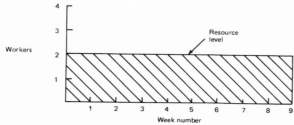

Network Information						Resource Loading Chart									
Act. No.	Dur.	No. Workers	ES	LF	Slack	Week Number									
						1	2	3	4	5	6	7	8	9	
1-2	4	1	0	4	0	[/	/	/	/]						
1-4	5	1	0	8	3	[		/	/	/	/	/]			
1-3	3	1	0	7	4	[/	/	/				]			
2-4	4	1	4	8	0				[/	/	/	/]			
3-4	1	2	3	8	4				[				]	2]	
Workers Required						2	2	2	2	2	2	2	2	2	
Workers Available						2	2	2	2	2	2	2	2	2	

Optimum schedule

Histogram of fixed resource limit—2 workers

Figure 5-2 Resource-constrained project

The two examples above give an overview of the nature of the scheduling problem and the methods that might be used to seek an optimal solution. Unfortunately, trial-and-error methods must be limited to problems with few activities and few resource categories. As activity and resource categories are added, the number of combinations and feasible schedules goes up at an increasing rate. Since trial-and-error methods are only useful for explanation and trivial problems, a systematic procedure is needed to develop a realistic and efficient schedule.

MATHEMATICAL ALGORITHM

The ideal procedure would be a pure mathematical algorithm for determining an *optimal* schedule. Given an objective function such as minimizing project duration or minimizing the level of resources, the management scientist would logically consider the linear programming technique to seek an optimal schedule. Although linear programming formulations of the problem have been developed,* this powerful technique is not practical in project-resource-scheduling problems. The basic reason for the impracticality of linear programming and other mathematical algorithms, such as integer programming, branch and bound, or dynamic programming lies in the combinatorial nature of the problem. The number of possible combinations within the preestablished network and resource boundary constraints makes even computer solution impractical. The iterative process of testing the number of feasible solutions that can arise from shifting start and finish time, slack times, resource availabilities, and project duration is impractical in terms of the amount of required computer time. The combinatorial problem also presents computer capacity and setup problems. Small networks of 25 activities, 3 different types of resources, and 50 time units might require as many as 4,000 constraint equations for a linear programming solution. Finally, any changes required after the project begins mean recomputing the entire resource schedule. Since mathematical algorithms appear to be impractical because of the combinatorial problem, heuristic methods along with the computer seem to be the next best thing.

HEURISTIC SCHEDULING

Recently the potential savings and the need to plan and control resource use have provided the impetus for a great research effort in heuristic resource scheduling. Today the word heuristic means "decision rule"—thus heuristic scheduling is scheduling by decision rules. The decision rules are intuitive rules developed from dealing repeatedly with the same problem. They are sometimes called rules of thumb or priority rules. Heuristic techniques are characteristically easy to apply and computation is minimized. Heuristic techniques *do not guarantee optimal results*; rather, they

---

* See D. Fulkerson, "A Network Flow Computation for Project Cost Curves," *Management Science* VII (January 1961): 167–78; J. Kelly, "Critical Path Planning and Scheduling: Mathematical Basis," *Operations Research* IX (May–June 1961): 296–320; J.J. Moder and C.R. Phillips, *Project Management with CPM and PERT* (New York: Van Nostrand Reinhold Co., 1970), pp. 206–35; J. Wiest and F. Levy, *A Management Guide to PERT/CPM* (Englewood Cliffs, N.J.: Prentice Hall, 1969), pp. 124–25.

are used to improve on current methods of allocating resources in large networks. In project management, heuristic scheduling generally requires a computer, although manual calculation is feasible on networks as large as 100 activities, 3 resources, and 60 time units.

A computer program is written which applies the decision rules to achieve a satisfactory schedule. It cannot be overemphasized that the efficiency of a schedule depends on the rules selected; the rules establish the schedule. The efficiency of the rules, in turn, depends on several other factors. The most important are the number of activities in the network, project duration, level of resource used, number of different resources used, number of parallel paths, and density of interlocking activities. Because all of these factors influence scheduling efficiency and since different sets of rules yield different results, it is customary to consider more than one set of scheduling rules to ensure that the final schedule used is reasonable in terms of project duration, resource levels, and fluctuations.

HEURISTIC SCHEDULING SYSTEMS

Different heuristic scheduling systems are used for time-constrained projects and for resource-constrained projects. The systems are simple in concept but tedious to calculate without computer assistance. Understanding the underlying principles is important if the systems are to be used intelligently. For example, project managers must be able to interpret output and explain to others why things must happen when they are scheduled. Also, to be able to select among the various features in a computer software program requires considerable understanding of the method used; this is also true for interpreting the results. For people who decide to write their own set of heuristics for manual or computer scheduling, a thorough understanding of the methods is imperative.

TIME-CONSTRAINED SCHEDULING SYSTEMS

The standard PERT/CPM network usually produces an uneven resource profile over the project duration. The implicit assumption is that, for practical purposes, resources are unlimited. The scheduling objective is to reduce the peak resource requirements to a profile that is as flat as possible, since the resource pool must be large enough to cover the maximum demand for the resource. Most heuristic leveling programs begin with an early start schedule and attempt to level the resources by utilizing slack. Early work on resource leveling was carried on concurrently by two management science teams—the Burgess and Killebrew team and the Levy,

Thompson and Wiest team.* Each team developed a computer system for leveling project resources; although there are minor differences, the approaches are similar.

The Burgess-Killebrew method uses the sum of the squares as a measure of scheduling effectiveness. The sum of the squares is computed in two steps. First, find the number of activities in progress in a time period and square this number. Second, add the squares for all the periods in the project. This sum for all the periods in the network is the measure of scheduling effectiveness.† The smaller the sum, the lower the resource profile and the better the scheduling effectiveness.

The leveling procedure uses simple rules:

1. Determine the early start schedule and the sum of its squares. Beginning with time period one, right shift an activity with slack to start one period later.

2. Check the sum of the squares for the project. If the sum does not increase, continue the process until the slack is used up. If the sum increases or if slack is used up, hold the previous position of this activity; then select another activity and repeat the above process.

3. When all of the activities in the project have been tested and the shifts made, the whole process can be repeated, since the starting times of some of the activities have changed and other shifts may lower the sum of the squares. The total process is repeated until no shifts in the network are possible.

Although this method may not provide an optimum schedule, experience indicates that the procedure has a high probability of coming very near the optimum (see Woodworth & Willie‡ for an extension of this method). The scheduling efficiency of this system depends on the order in which the activities are selected to be shifted. For this reason, it is advisable to have

* A.R. Burgess and J.B. Killebrew, "Variation in Activity Level on a Cyclical Arrow Diagram," *Journal of Industrial Engineering* XIII (March–April 1962): 76-83; and F.K. Levy, G.L. Thompson, and J.D. Wiest, "Multi-Ship, Multi-Shop Smoothing Program," *Naval Research Logistics Quarterly* IX (March 1962): 37-44.

† In multiresource projects the sum of the squares is computed for each resource. The number of activities is replaced with the *quantity of resource* being used in the selected period.

‡ B.M. Woodworth and C.J. Willie, "A Heuristic Algorithm for Resource Leveling in Multi-Project, Multi-Resource Scheduling," *Decision Sciences* VI (July 1975): 525-40.

a priority scheme for determining the order in which activities are selected, for example, ease of making the resource available or the cost of the resource.

The Levy, Thompson, and Wiest method uses the following procedure to level resources:

1. Begin with an early start schedule and profile.

2. Identify activities in progress during peak period(s). Randomly select one that has adequate slack to shift beyond the peak and schedule it in a period beyond the peak.

3. Identify the new resource peak(s). Repeat step 2. Continue this process until the peak(s) can no longer be reduced.

Since this system uses a random process to select the activity to shift and the amount it will be shifted, it is advisable to run the program several times to identify the most efficient system.

Today most major computer firms use a refined version of at least one of these methods; the programs will handle multiresource and multiproject conditions and are about equal in scheduling effectiveness. Although the discussion here was limited to a single project and resource, the principles are easily extended to handle several resources and projects simultaneously. Although both systems have had considerable application, time-constrained problems represent only a small proportion of the projects found in actual practice.

RESOURCE-CONSTRAINED SCHEDULING SYSTEMS

Resource-constrained projects represent about ninety percent of the projects dealt with in practice. (Some firms, however, must deal exclusively with time-constrained projects.) Two heuristic methods have been developed to schedule resource-constrained projects; they are the serial and the parallel methods.

Serial Method

This method schedules activities one at a time off an ordered priority list made up by following priority rules such as early start, least slack, and *i – j* sequence. Activities are taken from the list one at a time and the resources scheduled. When an activity is reached where adequate resources are not available in the resource pool, the start time is delayed until an activity already scheduled is finished and releases the resources. Sometimes rescheduling rules are used when resources are not available for scheduling; this changes the order of the list. When an activity is delayed from its expected start time because resources are unavailable, the following activities in the chain must have their expected times increased also.

Parallel Method

This method schedules on a period-by-period (week-by-week) basis and deals with *all* activities that are eligible for scheduling in that period. The priority of scheduling within a given period follows a set of priority rules such as minimum total slack and duration time. These priority rules establish the order in which eligible activities for the period are examined to see if they can be scheduled. Activities are scheduled if resources are available. If resources are not available, the activity is delayed until the next unit of time when it is then reconsidered. Some parallel methods allow rescheduling of activities when the demand for resources exceeds those available in the pool; that is, activities previously scheduled and carried into the current period being scheduled can be rescheduled if adequate slack exists.

Note that in both the serial and the parallel methods the relative importance of the activity may change as a result of the schedule. For example, noncritical tasks can become critical, while in some cases where the resource level is fixed, critical activities can become noncritical.

Example of the Serial Method. To keep the example relatively simple and to focus attention on methods and heuristics, the following assumptions will be used in both the serial and parallel problems:

1. The original sequential relationships of the network cannot be violated.

2. An activity can be scheduled to start at any time between its early start time (*ES*) and its late start time (*LS*). For critical activities the *ES* and *LS* values are identical.

3. Scheduling eligibility of each activity is determined by heuristics.

4. Activity resource level remains constant for the activity duration time.

5. Once an activity is scheduled it continues without interruption until it is completed.

If resource levels are fixed, the project duration time must be flexible. Hence, resource scheduling strives to minimize project duration time without exceeding the resource limit.

The network for the serial method problem is found in Figure 5-3. In this project the number of crews is limited to three and the project duration can be increased if the three crews are not adequate.

Network Output Sheet

Act.	Dur.	Res.	ES	EF	LS	LF	TS
1-2	3	2	0	3	0	3	0
1-3	2	1	0	2	2	4	2
2-4	4	1	3	7	4	8	1
2-5	4	2	3	7	3	7	0
2-6	3	1	3	6	8	11	5
3-5	3	2	2	5	4	7	2
4-6	3	1	7	10	8	11	1
5-6	4	2	7	11	7	11	0

Event Table

Event	ET
1	0
2	3
3	2
4	7
5	7
6	11

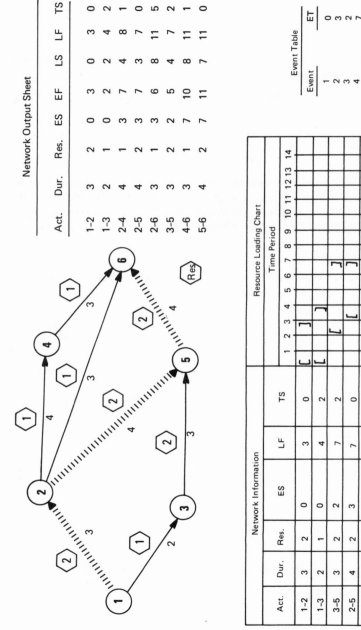

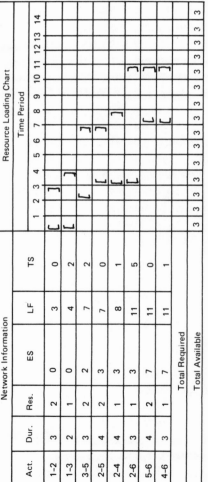

Figure 5-3   Serial method of scheduling a resource-constrained project

Heuristic 1. The following rules will be used to determine the scheduling priority list:

(1) early start time

(2) least total slack

(3) smallest duration time

(4) maximum resource level

(5) activity number $(i - j)$

The loading chart in Figure 5-3 was derived from applying these rules. The data on the left come from the Network Output Sheet. Note that the activities are ordered with early start as the first rule, least slack next, and so on. As the scheduling process is carried out, observe how the rank of the activities on the list determines the schedule. Total activity slack can be recomputed by the following equation:

$$TS = LF - (ES + t_e)$$

The loading (bar) chart is useful in the manual development of the resource schedule; the brackets indicate the interval in which the resource should be scheduled. The event table is used to keep track of the revised event times.

Heuristic 2. The following rules are used to schedule activities:

1. Moving down the list developed by Heuristic 1, attempt to schedule activities on their respective early starts.

2. If resources are not available, and slack exists, delay the schedule until the earliest feasible time when adequate resources do exist.

3. If slack does not exist, and resources are not available, schedule to minimize project delay.

Figure 5-4 presents these rules in a flowchart.

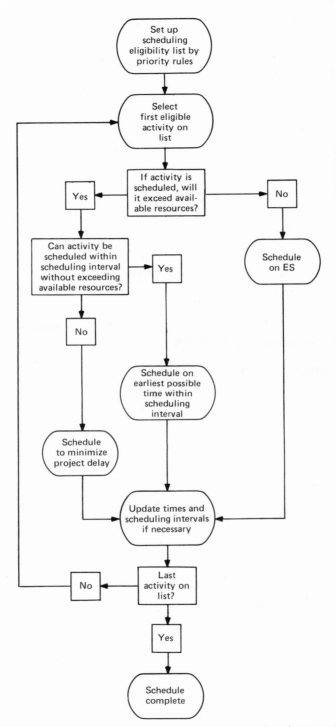

Figure 5-4 Serial method flowchart for resource-constrained problems (Adapted from
Network Analysis in Project Management, **by K.G. McLaren and E.L. Buesnel, pp. 129.
Used with permission of Cassell Ltd., England)**

Scheduling Procedure. The step-by-step scheduling procedure given below demonstrates the project manager's use of Heuristic 2.

1. The first activity on the list is activity 1-2:

Schedule activity 1-2   (No delay)
Update   (None required)

2. The next eligible activity is 1-3.

Schedule activity 1-3   (No delay)
Update   (None required)

3. The third eligible activity is 3-5. Since scheduling this activity on its early start time, 2, would cause an overload, the activity is delayed one week to time 3. The effect of this delay is to reduce the slack time for that segment of the chain. Note that if resources are indeed constrained, the slack time for activity 1-3 is also reduced one week. (To reduce the detail of the problems, we shall not update activities which have already been scheduled.) The expected event time for event 3 is also changed:

Schedule activity 3-5   (No delay)
Update   activity 3-5   ($ES = 3, TS = 1$)
Update   event   3   ($ET = 3$)

The loading chart in Figure 5-5 gives the results of scheduling the first three activities on the list.

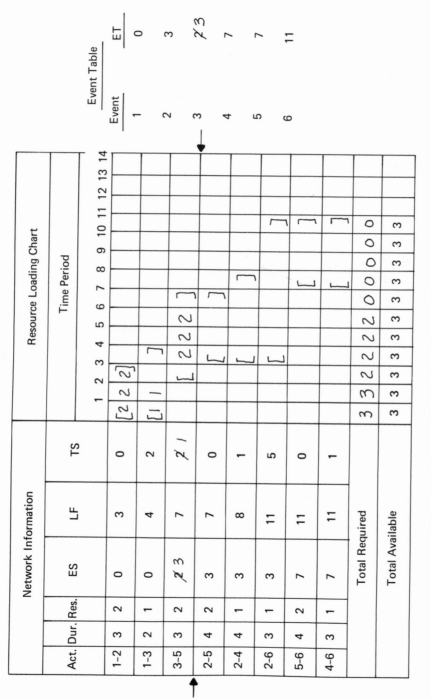

Figure 5-5   Resource loading chart (serial method)

4. The next eligible activity is 2-5. Scheduling this activity forces us to evoke the third scheduling rule which tells us to minimize the delay when adequate slack and resources are not available. Since scheduling activity 2-5 at any time before week 6 would cause us to exceed the three-crew limit, activity 2-5 is scheduled at the end of week 6, which causes a three-week delay in the project. Figure 5-6 depicts by means of dashed brackets the changes which then occur in the schedule interval of unscheduled activities. Note the number of updating changes that must take place (by now the value of a computer in heuristic scheduling should be evident):

Schedule activity 2-5   (3-week delay)

Update   activity 2-5 $(ES = 6, LF = 10, TS = 0)$
Update   activity 2-4 $(LF = 11, TS = 4)$
Update   activity 2-6 $(LF = 14, TS = 8)$
Update   activity 5-6 $(ES = 10, LF = 14)$
Update   activity 4-6 $(LF = 14, TS = 4)$

Update   event   4 $(ET = 11)$
Update   event   5 $(ET = 10)$
Update   event   6 $(ET = 14)$

Since the project end date has been delayed, the natural question at this point is, can we go back and look for rescheduling opportunities which might give a better schedule? In this case the answer is no, since the heuristics do not include rescheduling opportunities. In practice, however, more sophisticated programs use "look-back" scheduling rules when the original project due date is delayed.

5, 6, 7, 8. The remaining steps are straightforward:

Schedule activity 2-4   (No additional delay)
Schedule activity 2-6   (No additional delay)
Schedule activity 5-6   (No additional delay)
Schedule activity 4-6   (No additional delay)

Update   activity 2-6 $(ES = 7, TS = 4)$
Update   activity 4-6 $(ES = 10, TS = 1)$

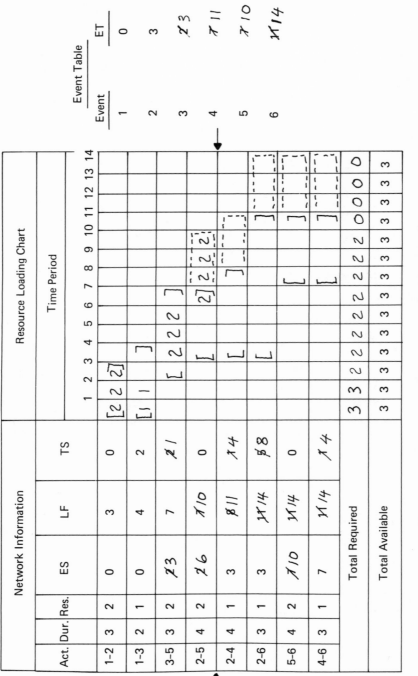

Figure 5-6   Loading chart showing changes (serial method)

Figure 5-7 exhibits the completed loading chart. In no period has the three- crew limit been exceeded. However, given the order and schedule rules and the three-crew constraint, it was necessary to delay the project three weeks beyond the original planning estimate of eleven weeks. The schedule developed from the final loading chart is presented in Table 5-1.

TABLE 5-1. RESOURCE LOADING SCHEDULE (three-crew limit).

Activity	Duration	Resource	Start	Finish
1-2	3	2	0	3
1-3	2	1	0	2
2-4	4	1	3	7
2-5	4	2	6	10
2-6	3	1	7	10
3-5	3	2	3	6
4-6	3	1	10	13
5-6	4	2	10	14

Example of the Parallel Method. Since the parallel method schedules on a period-by-period basis, the heuristics cover only the period being scheduled—not the total project as in the serial method. For example, in the serial method problems we used early start as the first rule and minimum total slack as the second rule. In the parallel method the early start rule is eliminated because each period (beginning with time period zero) is examined separately, and any activity that has its early start in that period will be considered as part of the eligible set. Since the parallel method takes care of the early start rule automatically, total slack is often the first rule for a particular period in this method.

It is important to remember that in parallel scheduling the heuristics cover only the period being examined. Essentially, there are only two steps to this method:

1. Schedule dummy activities first. Then attempt to schedule eligible activities for the selected period *t* at their earliest time using selected heuristics—with the exception that partially completed activities have first priority.

2. If resources are not adequate, remove noncritical activities that are currently *active* (partially completed) from the schedule. Attempt to re-schedule all eligible activities using selected heuristics. (This violates assumption 5 given earlier)

Resource Loading Chart

Network Information

Act.	Dur.	Res.	ES	LF	TS
1-2	3	2	0	3	0
1-3	2	1	0	4	2
3-5	3	2	2 3	7	2 1
2-5	4	2	3 6	7 10	0
2-4	4	1	3	8 11	5 4
2-6	3	1	8 7	11 14	6 4
5-6	4	2	7 10	11 14	0
4-6	3	1	7 10	11 14	4 1

Time Period

	1	2	3	4	5	6	7	8	9	10	11	12	13	14
1-2	[2	2	2]											
1-3	[1	1	1]											
3-5			[2	2	2	2]								
2-5							2]	2	2	2				
2-4			[1	1	1	1]								
2-6				[1	1	1]								
5-6							[	1	1	1	2	2	2	2]
4-6							[	1	1	1	1	1	1]	
Total Required	3	3	2	3	3	3	3	3	3	3	3	3	3	2
Total Available	3	3	3	3	3	3	3	3	3	3	3	3	3	3

Event Table

Event	ET
1	0
2	3
3	2 3
4	7 11
5	7 10
6	11 14

Figure 5-7 Completed loading chart (serial method)

The network for this problem is found in Figure 5-8. The number of crews is limited to a maximum of seven. If necessary, the project duration can be extended. The following order and schedule rules will be used to develop the resource schedule.

Heuristic 1. The eligibility for scheduling an unscheduled activity in a particular period will be determined by the following rules:

(1) minimum total slack

(2) smallest duration

(3) maximum resource level

(4) $i - j$ sequence

Heuristic 2. All activities in the set for the period being examined are either *active* activities that are partially completed or *unscheduled* activities that are eligible to start in the period being examined. Wiest has noted that it sometimes is possible to remove an *active*, noncritical scheduled activity from the schedule and use the released resources to improve resource utilization by scheduling a critical activity.* The heuristics used in this example will follow the flowchart shown in Figure 5-9.

Scheduling Procedure. The period-by-period scheduling procedure for the example problem is given below.

Time 0-1. The first week has three eligible activities which can be scheduled. Their priority is established by the heuristic 1 order rule of minimum total slack; hence the first activity to be examined is activity 1-2, the second is 1-3, and the third is 1-4. Adequate resources exist to schedule all three activities.

Schedule activity 1-2 (No delay)

Schedule activity 1-3 (No delay)

Schedule activity 1-4 (No delay)

Update   (None required)

Time 1-2. No change in the schedule is required. The eligible activities are already *active* in the schedule; that is, the schedule for this time period

---

* J.D. Wiest, "A Heuristic Model for Scheduling Large Projects with Limited Resources," *Management Science* XIII (February 1967): B-359–B-377.

Network Output Sheet

Act.	Dur.	Res.	ES	EF	LS	LF	TS
1-2	3	1	0	3	0	3	0
1-3	2	4	0	2	2	4	2
1-4	2	2	0	2	5	7	5
2-4	4	4	3	7	3	7	0
2-5	2	3	3	5	7	9	4
3-4	3	3	2	5	4	7	2
3-6	3	1	2	5	8	11	6
3-7	4	2	2	6	8	12	6
4-5	2	4	7	9	7	9	0
4-7	3	4	7	10	9	12	2
5-7	3	3	9	12	9	12	0
6-7	1	4	5	6	11	12	6

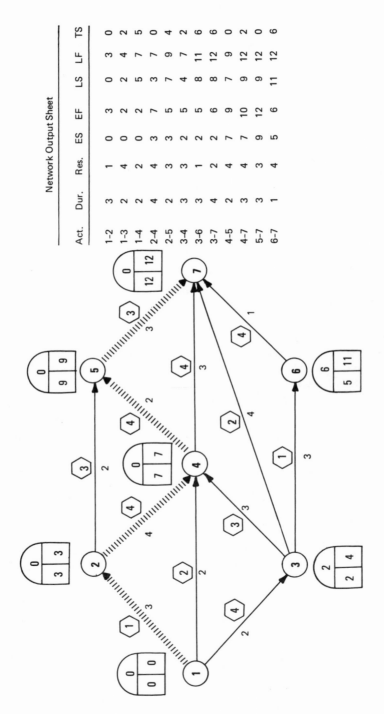

Figure 5-8 Parallel method of scheduling a resource-constrained project

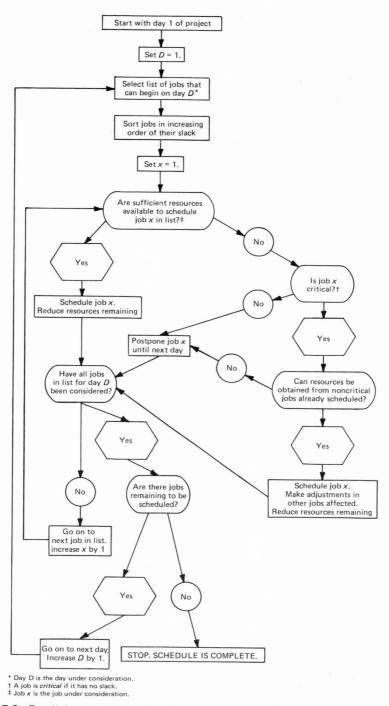

* Day D is the day under consideration.
† A job is *critical* if it has no slack.
‡ Job *x* is the job under consideration.

Figure 5-9 Parallel method flowchart for resource-constrained problems (From Jerome D. Wiest, Ferdinand K. Levy, *A Management Guide to PERT/CPM: With GERT/PDM/DCPM and other Networks*, 2nd ed., © 1977, p. 114. Reprinted by permission of Prentice-Hall, Inc., Englewood Cliffs, New Jersey.)

is made up entirely of partially completed activities. Recall from the scheduling rules that partially completed activities have first priority unless rescheduling is necessary and possible.

Time 2-3. Activity 1-2 is still active. Activities 3-4, 3-6, and 3-7 are added to the eligibility list by their respective priority.

Schedule activity 3-4   (No delay)

Schedule activity 3-6   (No delay)

Schedule activity 3-7   (No delay)

Update   (None required)

The loading chart in Figure 5-10 shows the results of scheduling through week 3.

Time 3-4. In this time period activities 3-4, 3-6, and 3-7 are active (partially completed) and have slack. Activities 2-4 and 2-5 are added to the priority list. Any attempt to schedule activities 2-4 or 2-5 fails because an overload results. The second scheduling rule, which allows rescheduling, must be evoked, that is, can noncritical activities that are currently active (3-4, 3-6, 3-7) be rescheduled so the critical activity (2-4) can be scheduled? The answer is yes. Remove activities 3-4, 3-6, and 3-7 from the active schedule and place them in the priority list developed by the order rules for time 3-4. The priority list is given below (assuming scheduling at the earliest possible time):

ACTIVITY	DURATION	RESOURCE	TS
2-4	4	4	0
3-4	3	3	1
2-5	2	3	4
3-6	3	1	5
3-7	4	2	5

Network Information						Resource Loading Chart													
						Time Period													
Act.	Dur.	Res.	ES	LF	TS	1	2	3	4	5	6	7	8	9	10	11	12	13	14
1-2	3	1	0	3	0	[1	1	1]											
1-3	2	4	0	4	2	[4	4		]										
1-4	2	2	0	7	5	[2	2					]							
2-4	4	4	3	7	0				[			]							
2-5	2	3	3	9	4				[					]					
3-4	3	3	2	7	2			[3	3	3		]							
3-6	3	1	2	11	6			[1	1	1						]			
3-7	4	2	2	12	6			[2	2	2	2						]		
4-5	2	4	7	9	0								[	]					
4-7	3	4	7	12	2								[				]		
5-7	3	3	9	12	0										[		]		
6-7	1	4	5	12	6						[						]		
Scheduled Crews						7	7	7	6	6	2								
Available Crews						7	7	7	7	7	7	7	7	7	7	7	7	7	7

Event Table

Event	ET
1	0
2	3
3	2
4	7
5	9
6	5
7	12

Figure 5-10 Parallel method loading chart through period 3

Now the first activity scheduled is 2-4. The next activity scheduled at its earliest time is 3-4. No other assignments are possible. The following operations take place.

Remove   activity 3-4
Remove activity   3-6
Remove   activity 3-7

Schedule activity 2-4   (No delay)
Schedule activity 3-4   (No delay)

Update   activity 2-5 $(ES = 4, TS = 3)$
Update   activity 3-6 $(ES = 4, TS = 4)$
Update   activity 3-7 $(ES = 4, TS = 4)$
Update   activity 6-7 $(ES = 7, TS = 4)$

Update   event   6 $(ET = 7)$

Figure 5.11 displays the results of scheduling and updating. Note that the *ES* of activity 6-7 is delayed two weeks because of the delay of its predecessor activity (3-6).

Time 4-5. Since those activities which are active (2-4, 3-4) take up all the available resources and since other activities have slack, no change in schedule is necessary:

Schedule   (No change)

Update   activity 2-5 $(ES = 5, TS = 2)$
Update   activity 3-6 $(ES = 5, TS = 3)$
Update   activity 3-7 $(ES = 5, TS = 3)$
Update   activity 6-7 $(ES = 8, TS = 3)$

Update   event   6 $(ET = 8)$

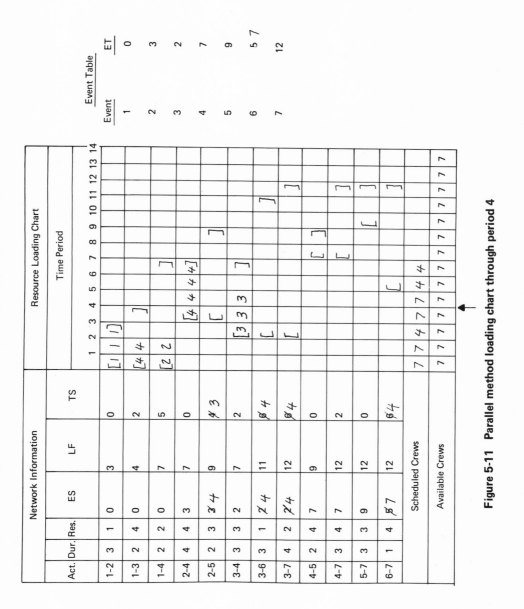

Figure 5-11 Parallel method loading chart through period 4

Time 5-6.

Schedule activity 2-5 (No delay)

Update activity 3-6 ($ES = 6, TS = 2$)

Update activity 3-7 ($ES = 6, TS = 2$)

Update activity 6-7 ($ES = 9, TS = 2$)

Update event   6 ($ET = 9$)

Time 6-7. No schedule change is necessary.

Update activity 3-6 ($ES = 7, TS = 1$)

Update activity 3-7 ($ES = 7, TS = 1$)

Update activity 6-7 ($ES = 10, TS = 1$)

Update event   6 ($ET = 10$)

Figure 5-12 shows the results of scheduling and updating.

Time 7-8. At this point four activities are eligible to be scheduled. Their priority by the order rules is shown below:

ACTIVITY	DURATION	RESOURCE	TS
4-5	2	4	0
3-6	3	1	1
3-7	4	2	1
4-7	3	4	2

Activity 4-5 is scheduled first. Activities 3-6 and 3-7 can also be scheduled. Activity 4-7 is delayed.

Schedule activity 4-5 (No delay)

Schedule activity 3-6 (No delay)

Schedule activity 3-7 (No delay)

Update activity 4-7 ($ES =8, TS = 1$)

See Figure 5-12 for these changes in the loading chart.

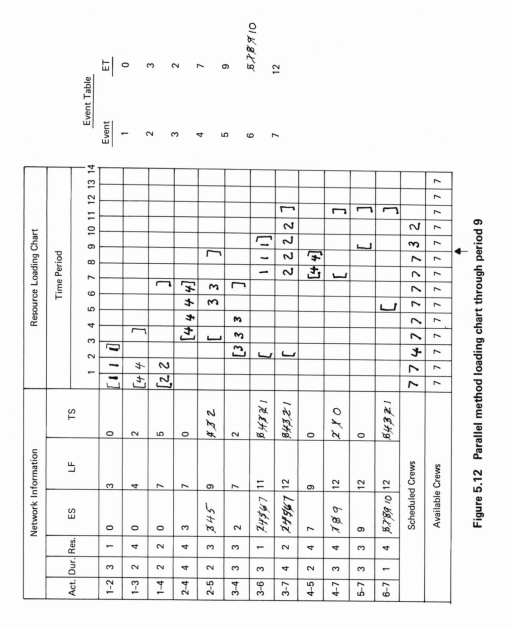

Figure 5.12 Parallel method loading chart through period 9

Time 8-9. No change in schedule.

Update   activity 4-7 ($ES = 9$, $TS = 0$)

The completed schedule through week 9 is found in the loading chart of Figure 5-12.

Time 9-10. Activities 4-7 and 5-7 are both critical in the resource schedule, that is, both have zero slack. Only activity 4-7 can be scheduled. Since the resource level is fixed, the project will have to be delayed—to schedule activity 5-7 would exceed the limit of seven crews. (Note that the procedure does not acknowledge this fact until activity 5-7 is actually scheduled late—see time 11-12 below.)

Schedule activity 4-7 (No delay)

Update   activity 5-7 ($ES = 10$, $LF = 13$, $TS = 0$)

Update   activity 6-7 ($LF = 13$, $TS = 2$)

Update   event   7 ($ET = 13$)

Since we are not using rescheduling heuristics for situations where the project completion date is extended, we will not update the LF times of those activities already scheduled. However, a computer program would do this.

Time 10-11. No schedule change is necessary.

Update   activity 5-7 ($ES = 11$, $LF = 14$, $TS = 0$)

Update   activity 6-7 ($ES = 11$, $LF = 14$, $TS = 2$)

Update   event   7 ($ET = 14$)

Time 11-12.

Schedule activity 5-7 (Project delayed 2 weeks)

Update   activity 6-7 ($ES = 12$, $TS = 1$)

Time 12-13 and 13-14.

Schedule activity 6-7 (2-week delay)

Figure 5-13 presents the completed resource loading chart. Note that the resource constraint of seven crews forces a two-week delay in project completion using the heuristics given.

This completes the basic generalized procedural aspects of heuristic scheduling using both serial and parallel methods. Each method is capable of handling resource-constrained problems. Although the heuristic methods described are relatively simple, they are powerful and capable of producing near optimal results. Field and experimental tests suggest that the peak resource level of an early start schedule can be reduced about 25–50 percent, while project slippage will not usually exceed 5–10 percent, by using heuristics such as those discussed in this chapter.

SCHEDULING EFFICIENCY

Since different heuristics yield different schedules, it is convenient to have some method to compare different scheduling rules to determine which ones produce the most efficient resource schedule. The two most frequent criteria used to measure scheduling efficiency are resource utilization and project slippage. Resource utilization is important since idle resources are costly. Project slippage is significant in terms of customer good will, penalty costs, and interfacing with other projects or plans. Resource utilization can be defined simply as the ratio of total resources scheduled for the duration of the project to those available for the duration. In equation notation, resource utilization can be expressed as follows:

$$U_j = \frac{\sum\limits_{i=0}^{i=D} R_i}{(D \times L)}$$

where

U_j = Resource utilization ratio
    for resource j

$\sum\limits_{i=0}^{i=D} R_i$ = Sum of scheduled resource
    for project duration

D = Project duration (after scheduling) or
    scheduling period

L = Maximum level of resource available during
    any period of the project duration (D)

Network Information						Resource Loading Chart													
						Time Period													
Act.	Dur.	Res.	ES	LF	TS	1	2	3	4	5	6	7	8	9	10	11	12	13	14
1-2	3	1	0	3	0	[1	1	1]											
1-3	2	4	0	4	2	[4	4		]										
1-4	2	2	0	7	5	[2	2					]							
2-4	4	4	0	7	0				[4	4	4	4]							
2-5	2	3	~~3~~ ~~4~~ 5	9	~~4~~ ~~3~~ ~~2~~				[		3	3		]					
3-4	3	3	2	7	2			[3	3	3		]							
3-6	3	1	~~2~~ ~~4~~ ~~5~~ ~~6~~ 7	11	~~6~~ ~~4~~ ~~3~~ ~~2~~ 1			[					1	1	1	]			
3-7	4	2	~~2~~ ~~4~~ ~~5~~ ~~6~~ 7	12	~~6~~ ~~4~~ ~~3~~ ~~2~~ 1			[					2	2	2	2	]		
4-5	2	4	7	9	0								[4	4]					
4-7	3	4	~~7~~ ~~8~~ 9	12	~~2~~ ~~1~~ 0								[		4	4	4]		
5-7	3	3	9	~~12~~ ~~13~~ 14	0										[		3]	3	3
6-7	1	4	~~5~~ ~~7~~ ~~8~~ ~~9~~ ~~10~~ ~~11~~ 12	~~12~~ ~~13~~ 14	~~6~~ ~~4~~ ~~3~~ ~~2~~ ~~1~~/~~2~~ 1						[						]	4	
Scheduled Crews						7	7	4	7	7	7	7	7	7	7	6	7	7	3
Available Crews						7	7	7	7	7	7	7	7	7	7	7	7	7	7

Event Table

Event	ET
1	0
2	3
3	2
4	7
5	9
6	~~5~~ ~~7~~ ~~8~~ ~~9~~ 10
7	~~12~~ ~~13~~ 14

Figure 5-13 Parallel method loading chart through period 14

For example, the ratio for the project schedule in Figure 5-13 is computed as follows. The sum of the scheduled resources is 90 crew days and the total crew availability is 98 (14 x 7) crew days. The resource utilization ratio for the project—given the heuristics used—is 90/98 or 92 percent. Since the efficiency of specific heuristics depends on the project itself, and each project is different, empirical verification of which heuristics are best is difficult to obtain. A great deal of field work and laboratory experiments suggests that at least one rule consistently does well in terms of resource utilization and project slippage. The research of Findley, Wiest, and Pascoe all agree that project slippage and idle resources are minimized by using the *minimum total slack rule* as the first rule when using the parallel method.* However, if other criteria are important for evaluating scheduling efficiency (that is, in-process inventory), the minimum slack rule may be far from best.† Thus, the importance of testing several heuristics to see which ones best meet the needs cannot be overemphasized. First set criteria for evaluating scheduling efficiency; then develop heuristics which yield schedules that move toward optimizing the criteria selected.

EXTENSIONS OF BASIC SERIAL AND PARALLEL METHODS

MULTIPLE RESOURCE PROJECTS

In practice managers often face projects and individual activities which demand the use of several different resources simultaneously. For example, one activity may require four carpenter crews, one unskilled labor crew, and one crane to complete the activity. Conditions which demand the use of several resources simultaneously increase the probability of delaying the project when the resource levels are fixed, since it is assumed that if one resource is not available, the activity cannot begin. Fortunately, all of the procedures outlined in the serial and parallel methods apply to multiple-resource problems. The only difference is that all resources for an activity must be allocated simultaneously—not separately.

VARIABLE-RESOURCE LEVELS

Fixed-resource levels place stringent restrictions on scheduling. Variable-resource levels help to increase resource utilization and reduce project slippage. For example, if a road contractor set the network time estimate

---

* L.G. Findley, "Toward the Development of a Complete Multiproject Scheduling System," in *Journal of Industrial Engineering*, vol. 19 (Oct. 1968) 505–15; J.D. Wiest, "A Heuristic Model for Scheduling Large Projects with Limited Resources," in *Management Science*, vol. 18 February 1967) B359-77; T.L. Pascoe, "Heuristic Methods for Allocating Resources," unpub. Ph.D. diss., Univ. of Cambridge, U.K. (1965).

† E.B. Talbot and J.H. Patterson, "Optimal Methods for Scheduling Projects Under Resource Constraints," in *Project Management Quarterly*, vol. 10 no. 4 (December 1979) 26-33.

for clearing one mile of land based on five bulldozers, the fact that one dozer is not available should not delay starting the job—although it is reasonable to expect that the project duration will be longer. Flexibility in scheduling is gained by flagging those activities which can be done with a smaller resource level than originally planned. To avoid reducing the resource (that is, labor or its equivalent) to an inefficient point, a threshold or minimum resource level is set. When the resources available fall below this minimum, it is not feasible to do the job and it is delayed.

Often a 70–80 percent minimum is used to avoid the difficulties of specifying a different level for each type of resource, such as carpenters, plumbers, or electricians. The effect of a minimum labor level on the activity duration time is difficult to assess; however, the use of man-days (weeks) as a base can help estimate the new activity time. For example, if a crew of 10 could complete the activity in 4 workdays or 40 man-days, a crew of 8 would still require 40 man-days, but 5 workdays. The same procedure can be used for equipment.

Most scheduling systems also allow the project manager to change the level of resources; that is, if it is known that additional resources will be available at a specific date, the manager can add this information to the computer input. This feature is used a great deal in practice.

SPLITTING

In project management, splitting means interrupting the completion of an activity by shifting the resource from an *active* activity to one of higher priority; when the higher priority activity is completed, the resource is returned so the interrupted activity can continue. In projects where the nature of the work does not require that the activities be worked from beginning to end without interruption, switching resources back and forth between activities facilitates increased resource utilization and reduced project slippage. Splitting often occurs when unskilled labor is utilized or in tasks considered as "fill-in work."

MULTIPROJECT RESOURCE SCHEDULING

Some firms have several projects running concurrently. In these multiproject firms the stakes are higher and the benefits or penalties for good or bad resource planning and scheduling become even more significant than in most single projects. For example, what would be the impact on the labor resource pool of a construction company if the company should win a particular contract management would like to bid on? Will existing labor be adequate to deal with the new project—given the completion date? Will current projects be delayed? Will layoffs be necessary? Will subcontracting help? If projects compete for the same resources, which project has priority? Multiproject managers must have the answers to such questions if they are to plan and schedule efficiently. The methods presented in this chapter are applicable to multiproject scheduling with only minor differences; each project is treated as if it were a fragnet (subnet) of one large project— even though each project is, in fact, independent.

To manage multiprojects, two or more projects must be connected to make one larger network. This is accomplished easily by creating a common start event and a common end event for all projects. A dummy activity is used to link each project to the common start event; similarly, a dummy activity is used to link each project to a common end event.

At least two additional bits of information are needed for multiproject resource scheduling. First, start dates must be established for each project. Multiproject organizations seldom start all of their projects at the same time; old ones are completed and new ones are added. By assigning times to the connecting dummy activities, the starting times of each project can be controlled. For example, to start Project B on week ten, a real-time dummy activity with a duration of ten weeks would precede the first event of Project B; the effect of this real-time dummy activity is the creation of a "waiting" activity. Second, finish times must be established for each project. Since at least one project will have a longest duration, it is necessary to assign completion times to projects with smaller durations. The purposes of assigning duration times to the dummy activities that link the project to the final end event are to *give each project equal weight or priority* when scarce resources are scheduled and to create a critical path with zero slack. All of this sounds more complicated than it really is.

Figure 5-14 is an example of a multiproject network. The common start event for all projects is event 1; the common end event is event 100. Dummy activities 1-10, 1-20, 1-30, 18-100, and 28-100, and 39-100 link the projects together. Dummy activity 1-10 has zero time duration, which means that Project 1 can start at time zero. Dummy activity 1-20 has a duration of five, which has the effect of not allowing Project 2 to start before time period five. Activity 1-30 delays Project 3 until time period seven.

The planning period "end" for all of the projects must be established. This may be the end of the year or anytime management desires. In most cases, however, the planning period end is set equal to the duration of the longest project—including the duration for the real-time dummy, if the dummy exists for the project. Note that this duration assumes unlimited resources. In Figure 5-14 Project 3 establishes the planning period end as twenty-one.

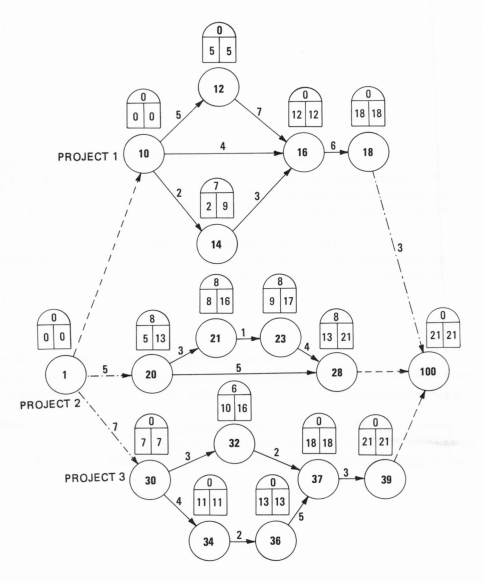

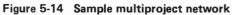

Figure 5-14 Sample multiproject network

Given the planning period end, dummy activities are used to give each project equal weight and create a critical path through each project that is zero. In Figure 5-14 Project 3 has the longest duration (21 periods); hence, dummy activity 39-100 is given a duration of zero. To give Project 1 an equal weight with Project 3, it is necessary to assign a duration of three to activity 18-100. Note that the critical path in Projects 1 and 3 have slack of zero. Project 2 has been left with a zero duration for activity 28-100 to demonstrate how this might change the priority of the project, and the critical path has a slack of eight time units. The slack of eight for Project 2 (see critical path) could have the effect of giving the project a lower priority when resources are scheduled because almost all resource scheduling systems use minimum slack as the first criterion for selecting which activity will be scheduled first.

A natural question at this point is, How do you know the duration times for the real time dummy activities *before* you compute the durations for all the projects? The answer is that you don't. Either you run all the projects through the computer to find the project duration for each project and then find the difference (slack) between the longest project and all others, or your computer program determines the durations of all the projects and automatically inserts durations which give the critical path of each project zero slack.

In summary, multiproject management requires the assignment of start times for each project by assigning a duration time to the dummy activity that links the project to the common start event. Completion times are set by assigning a duration time to the dummy activity that links the project to the common end event. The purpose of assigning completion times is to give each project equal weight or priority and to create a project critical path with a slack of zero. Of course, it is possible to create a higher priority for a project by assigning the end dummy activity with a duration larger than needed to make the critical path of the project have negative slack. Conversely, a lower priority can be created by assigning the end dummy activity a duration less than needed as we did in Project 2, activity 28-100.

STANDARDIZED NETWORKS

In the last few years the use of standardized networks has increased in multiproject organizations. Standardized networks can be used in organizations which do the same kind of work year in and year out even if each project is different. Such networks eliminate the need to draw new networks for each project. The manager simply reads down the list of activities and fills in the time estimate and the resource skill and quantity. If a particular activity does not exist in this project, the manager ignores it; the computer program builds the network, schedules the project, and develops the resource cost budget. Several organizations have found that a standardized network is easily understood by managers and eliminates a great deal of paper work. The U.S. Forest Service has found this approach very helpful. For example, one forest in the Pacific Northwest schedules approximately 150 timber sales per year using a standardized network; although each sale is different—especially in time estimates for activities—the standardized network is able to cover all of the 150 projects. State highway departments have also found standardized networks useful. A customized sawmill builder uses a standardized network to schedule the construction of new mills, to determine labor needs, and to set budgets. One project organization uses three standardized networks to cover approximately 99 percent of the projects they work with each year. Each project is a variation of one of the three networks. Selection of which network to use is obvious to all involved. Standard forms are used, and planning time has been slashed and most planning is done by first-line supervision.

In all cases the intent is to reap the benefits which usually accompany standardized networks:

1. Shift responsibility for input to lower levels in the organization

2. Reduction of input errors

3. Reduction of personnel planning time by as much as 80 percent

It is likely that standardized networks will become a very useful approach to manage some fabrication and construction firms which build similar products each year. Future developments are likely to make this approach to project management acceptable because of the large reduction in planning costs.

CONCLUSION

The author has found the planning and replanning of resources to be one of the most significant aspects of project management. So many things (for example, inflation) are beyond the project manager's control, but this is one area where the project manager does have the ability to manage. Those who truly understand the concepts and techniques discussed in this chapter should have very little trouble handling complex projects.

QUESTIONS

5-1. If a project is time constrained, we assume resources are unlimited. Conversely, if a project is resource constrained, we assume time is flexible. What do these two statements mean in practice?

5-2. What are the major scheduling problems in time-constrained and resource-constrained projects?

5-3. Why are heuristic scheduling methods used when mathematical optimizing procedures are available?

5-4. Give examples of heuristics used to schedule resource-constrained projects. Set your examples up in the priority or sequence in which they will be used. Why do you believe the sequence you have chosen will create an efficient schedule?

5-5. How is linking used in multiproject management to create a critical path with zero slack for a single project?

5-6. Are there any disadvantages to splitting in managing project resources?

EXERCISES

5-1. Below is network information provided by staff specialists:

ACTIVITY	DURATION	RESOURCE	ES	LS	EF	LF	SLACK
1-2	5	1	0	0	5	5	0
1-3	3	2	0	2	3	5	2
1-5	2	3	0	7	2	9	7
2-3	0	0	5	5	5	5	0
2-6	4	1	5	8	9	12	3
3-4	5	2	5	5	10	10	0
4-7	5	3	10	10	15	15	0
5-6	3	1	2	9	5	12	7
6-7	3	2	9	12	12	15	3

Schedule the project using the parallel method. Assume the resource pool is limited to *four*. Use a loading chart similar to those found in the chapter to set up your schedule.

The following heuristics and scheduling rules should be used:

1. *Heuristics.* The eligibility for scheduling an unscheduled activity in a particular period will be determined by the following heuristics:

   a. minimum slack
   b. smallest duration
   c. maximum resource level
   d. $i - j$ sequence

2. *Scheduling rules.* All activities in the set for the time period being examined are either *active* activities that are partially completed, or unscheduled activities that are eligible to be scheduled in the period being examined.

   a. Attempt to schedule eligible activities for the selected period at their earliest time using the heuristics—with the exception that partially completed activities have first priority.
   b. *If* resources are not adequate, remove noncritical activities that are currently active from the schedule. Attempt to reschedule all eligible activities using the heuristics. Remember to update slack before you reschedule.
   c. Splitting is not allowed, even though it might improve the solution.

List the order in which you scheduled each activity. What is the project **duration in your schedule? Which activities are critical?**

5-2. The following project information has been developed:

ACTIVITY	DURATION	RESOURCE	ES	LS	EF	LF	SLACK
1-2	3	1	0	0	3	3	0
1-5	2	4	0	6	2	8	6
2-3	2	4	3	3	5	5	0
2-4	5	2	3	9	8	14	6
3-4	4	2	5	10	9	14	5
3-6	4	4	5	5	9	9	0
4-7	1	3	9	14	10	15	5
5-7	0	0	2	15	2	15	13
5-9	6	1	2	8	8	14	6
6-7	6	1	9	9	15	15	0
6-8	2	2	9	15	11	17	6
7-10	3	3	15	15	18	18	0
8-10	1	2	11	17	12	18	6
9-10	4	2	8	14	12	18	6

Schedule the project using the parallel method. Assume the resource pool is limited to *five*. Use a loading chart to schedule the resources. Use the heuristics and scheduling rules found in exercise 5-1.

List the final order in which you schedule the activities. How does the project duration of your schedule compare with the duration found in the plan?

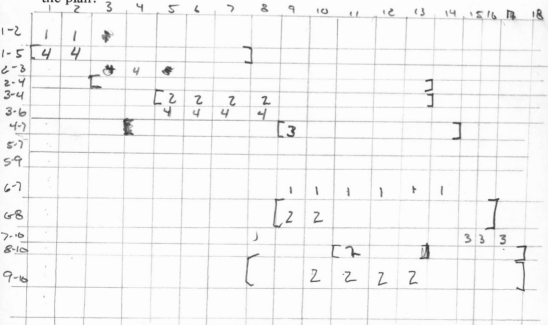

5-3. Given the network information below, schedule the project using the parallel method and assuming the resource pool is limited to *six*. Use the same heuristics and scheduling rules found in exercises 5-1 and 5-2. List the order in which you schedule the activities.

ACTIVITY	DURATION	RESOURCE	ES	LS	EF	LF	SLACK
1-2	3	3	0	3	3	6	3
1-3	2	4	0	0	2	2	0
1-4	4	2	0	1	4	5	1
2-7	6	3	3	6	9	12	3
3-5	1	2	2	6	3	7	4
3-6	4	1	2	2	6	6.	0
4-6	1	3	4	5	5	6	1
4-9	4	2	4	10	8	14	6
5-7	5	2	3	7	8	12	4
5-8	3	3	3	11	6	14	8
6-8	8	1	6	6	14	14	0
7-10	4	3	9	12	13	16	3
8-10	2	2	14	14	16	16	0
9-10	2	3	8	14	10	16	6

5-4. Use the information below to develop a schedule for the project. Assume the resource pool is limited to *seven*. Schedule by the parallel method and the rules found in exercise 5-1. List activities in the order in which you schedule them. Which activities are critical? What is the project duration? What is the efficiency of your schedule?

ACTIVITY	DURATION	RESOURCE
1-2	3	2
1-3	4	3
1-4	2	1
2-5	2	2
2-6	5	2
3-7	3	1
4-7	1	3
4-8	4	2
5-9	1	1
6-7	2	4
6-9	4	2
7-10	3	4
8-10	2	1
9-10	3	5

5-5. Finn Construction Company: You own a small construction company which specializes in finishing houses. Another contractor has subcontracted to you the job of finishing a house. The foundation, basic framework, and plumbing have been completed. Upon agreeing to terms, you sit down and analyze the problem confronting you.

Assuming carpenters and electricians are available, you can simultaneously install the wiring (2 workers for 3 days), lay the floors (1 worker for 4 days), hang the doors (2 workers for 1 day), and finish the exterior (3 workers for 5 days). After the wiring has been installed, you can finish the interior walls (3 workers for 3 days) and then hook up the electrical fixtures (2 workers for 1 day). Once the doors are hung you can install the windows (2 workers for 2 days). As soon as the exterior is finished you can make the necessary hookups to bring electricity in from the existing power lines (2 workers for 1 day).

You are faced with the following constraints. Electricians and carpenters are not allowed to work in areas other than those specifically related to their trade (electricians cannot do carpenters' work). The electricians will perform the following activities: install electrical wiring, hook up electrical fixtures, and hook up to existing power lines; the carpenters will perform the rest of the activities.

Assignment:

1. Draw the network assuming unlimited resources. What is the critical path?

2. If all the activities are scheduled at their early start, what is the level of resources needed each day? Is this an efficient method? Why?

Assume the firm only has two electricians and four carpenters available. Use the parallel method and the scheduling rules below to construct a schedule. (Use a loading chart format.) What is the duration time? What is the efficiency of this schedule?

Minimum slack
Minimum duration
Maximum resource
i
j

PART III
PROJECT PERFORMANCE AND CONTROL

This part examines some of the concerns project managers encounter once the project has actually been started. Measuring and controlling project performance is simple in concept but very difficult in practice, yet it must be done. Some method for determining the current status of the project is needed, which means data must be collected to facilitate comparing actual versus expected outcomes. When these data are collected, problem identification and analysis must take place. Problem analysis is followed by a step-by-step procedure for taking corrective action. Then the project manager must manage the updated situation. Periodically a new status report is generated and the controlling is repeated; this process continues until the project is completed.

Typically, after the project has been started certain types of problems occur because they were not given adequate attention by management before the project was given the go-ahead. For example, lack of top management support and unclear lines of authority and responsibility typically show up in the implementation phase. Some of these problems are discussed in the next chapter.

Finally, a generalized model for time and cost control is presented. Understanding the basics of this model should allow the reader to understand quickly the computer packages found in the real world of project management.

6
Project Implementation and Control

THIS CHAPTER provides some guidelines and methods for use in managing projects involving network-based techniques. It covers the problem of organizing for the project, describes updating and resource control reports, and, finally, discusses training for project management.

IMPLEMENTATION GUIDELINES

Some managers may prefer to use the network only to plan the project. Once the project begins the network drawing is rolled up and placed in a dusty corner. It has been said that 70 percent of the value of critical path methods is in developing the planning network. This may be true for small projects, projects that have a short duration, or projects that are repeated over and over. But where projects are large, of long duration, and relatively new and untried, using only the planning network (omitting scheduling and controlling) could result in catastrophic errors and blunders. Plans seldom materialize in every detail.

With critical path (or network-based) information systems, the project manager can get useful feedback information on project status, identifying potential problems and providing a solid basis for management decision making. The alternative of not using network-based information systems usually results in situations where management receives very little information and decisions are made on the basis of "gut feelings." In large projects where timing and coordination are important, "gut feelings" do not account for much. In such organizations management meetings typically ramble from one topic to the next and last for hours, and decisions are made on the basis of very little fact. In critical path information systems the network provides the medium for communication, assignment of responsibility, resource allocations, and cost control. All managers can receive the same information; problem areas are pinpointed. Assuming project status information is timely and accurate, management meetings have more direction and decisions will be more accurate and precise. Everyone in the organization can visualize how his or her actions will influence other departments or project duration.

Implementation and control of projects with network-based information systems demand a real commitment by management at all levels; a half-hearted, unenthusiastic attempt to use the system will never succeed. Overcoming resistance to change is always difficult. The first project using critical path systems should be selected carefully so the new system has a good chance of success. The system used should be as compatible as possible with existing systems. Participative management and task force approaches have been successful in gaining support for critical path systems. If the organization does not have the personnel skilled in network techniques, training classes may be used to develop the necessary skills, or outside consultants may assist in implementing and controlling the project.

Experience has shown that realizing the full potential of critical path systems can be hindered if management falls into four very common traps. First, time estimates should be arrived at by assuming normal conditions, for instance, equipment presently available, normal crews, five-day weeks, no overtime. If this approach is not used, management will face a situation of full capacity utilization but with no room to expedite the schedule after the project has started.

Second, time estimates are exactly that—estimates. Time estimates should mean that there is approximately a 50-50 chance of being either early or late. This does *not* mean there is 100 percent assurance that the activity will be completed by the estimated time; rather, there is only a 50 percent chance. If there is one sure way to ruin a planning system, it is for management to ask the worker for an activity time estimate and then turn around and demand a commitment to finish the work in that time. What happens the next time management asks for a time estimate? The same individual, remembering the last experience, will think of a time estimate, mentally add a cushion, and then give an estimate that has a near 100 percent assurance of being completed in the estimated time. Many good information-planning systems have met their demise when managers have failed to understand the clear distinction between estimates and commitments. Commitments should be used sparingly.

Third, finish dates should not enter into the development of the network plan and activity time estimates. To set a schedule date and work back usually ends up with a good deal of second guessing of which path will be critical and with adjustments in time estimates by changing the normal level of resources needed to complete the activity. After the planning network with time estimates is finished, management can go back and decide which activities *on the critical path* may need to be crashed to meet a scheduled date.

Finally, because of contractual arrangements with customers or other departments, top management may select milestones before the planning network is developed. This often results in milestones that do not even closely relate to those developed by the project task force which develops the network. If at all possible, let the milestones be identified from the network composed of work packages defined by the people responsible for getting the activities completed. Other traps exist; the four listed are merely the most common.

PROJECT AUTHORITY AND RESPONSIBILITY

Projects are usually implemented and completed by an interdisciplinary task force temporarily created for the duration of the project. This would be true regardless of the type of organization—product, service, or project. The task force is usually formed by two groups: the operating group which is directly responsible for getting the project completed within the resource and time constraints given, and the service group which collects project data and provides management reports. To be effective the task force must not only be saddled with the responsibility of getting the project completed but also with the authority to make it happen.

What is the best method for integrating the project and its task force into the current everyday operation of the organization?

The most successful way to integrate the new project management team with the current organization is to send out a directive that gives the following information:

(1) project manager

(2) project objectives

(3) authority and responsibility relationships that will exist between the project task force and other departments, such as marketing, finance, and operations, for example, (a) priority of project and (b) financial, labor, and equipment resources controlled by the project manager

The intent of the directive is to indicate clearly top-management support and to ensure coordination of diverse activities and groups. Even though the activities are segmented on the planning network, all of them must be coordinated and finally merged into the total system of the project. Because most projects involve interdisciplinary groups and many different departments or contractors working on the same activities, projects cut across organizational lines. This diversity of activities and groups requires tremendous coordination efforts if the project is to be completed successfully. The directive is the document which sets the stage for coordination of the project by showing top-management support and expected authority-responsibility relationships.

NETWORK-BASED INTEGRATED INFORMATION SYSTEM

Once management has created a receptive environment for network-based project management, developed network plans, and scheduled resources, both the project and the management control processes can begin. Fundamental to the control process is an information system which tells the project manager what is currently planned and scheduled, what has happened to date, and what future performance can be expected. By analyzing the reports generated by the information system, the project manager can decide on necessary courses of action.

For convenience of discussion, the network-based information system for project management can be segmented into two phases: information generated before the project begins and information generated after the project commences. Essentially, the first phase is the planning and scheduling phase, and the second phase is implementing and controlling. Information generated in the planning and scheduling phase usually includes the following:

(1) network times, slack, and critical path

(2) resource schedules for labor, equipment, and money

(3) breakdown of costs and budgets

Information generated from the implementing and controlling phase usually includes the following kinds of reports:

(1) current status by department, division, or organization

(2) problem analysis and corrective action reports

(3) management summary reports

Of course, in practice planning, scheduling, and controlling are a continual process. Once the project actually begins, replanning and rescheduling will be necessary as the project is implemented.

The information system described here was developed by space and defense contractors; this system received a major thrust in 1962 when the Department of Defense and the National Aeronautics and Space Administration published the *DOD and NASA Guide, PERT Cost System Design.* In a short while several government agencies—DOD, NASA, and Corps of Engineers—required contractors of large projects to use the PERT/Cost system to report progress and control cost. Although the information system is recognized as a valuable tool for project control, the problems of designing an information system for project management and then interfacing it with traditional control systems are sometimes difficult to overcome.

INFORMATION SYSTEM DESIGN AND INTERFACE CONSIDERATIONS

In designing an information system for project management, most control is directed toward time-oriented activities. This is a highly logical design philosophy for project management, since it is possible to gain good project control by assigning specific responsibility and authority to management to complete an activity within planned labor and equipment resources, a duration time, and a dollar budget. The information system can compare the planned versus the actual to find the variances in labor, equipment, time, and budget. Management can analyze these data and take corrective action. As logical and simple as this system sounds, problems can arise when managers attempt to integrate the system with traditional control systems which are directed toward a department, division, or total organization. This is especially true when management tries to make an activity-oriented cost system compatible with an already existing cost system set up by functions—marketing, finance, and production.

This switch of emphasis to activity and thus project control can cause organizational problems. Resistance to change and the extra effort required to accommodate the activity-oriented cost control system are not easy to overcome in practice. The usual approach to the cost accounting problem has been to develop an activity cost system that is a subsystem of the traditional cost system. Accompanying the activity cost system is an organization/activity matrix chart similar to the one shown in Figure 6-1. This chart can be used to assign project cost control within the larger functional organization. By "overlaying" the activity cost system on the traditional cost system, it is possible to overcome resistance to change, increase understanding and cooperation between the functional organization and the project management team, and achieve better overall project control.

Another problem associated with an activity-oriented cost system is the level of detail. The information requirements for an activity cost system are usually more extensive, since each activity becomes the near equivalent of a cost center; furthermore, the cost center is closed out when the activity is completed. Because detail can quickly destroy the system, it is common to divide the cost of the project into "work packages" of one or more related activities grouped together for cost-control purposes. This grouping of activities reduces the level of detail significantly, distributes the overhead more equitably, and assigns responsibility for cost more logically. The natural sequence of the activity-oriented network does not need to be altered when work packages are used. Work packages should probably consist of activities of no more than two months' duration or $100,000 of cost to be effective for cost control. However, at the other extreme, work packages should not be so small that the level of detail costs more than the value of the information derived. As a rule of thumb, the level of detail should be no more than is absolutely necessary.

Other problems associated with activity-oriented cost systems are those of joint and overhead costs. Sometimes several activities being performed at different times or locations will share costs; the problems of allocating such joint costs must be overcome. Again, the activity or work package can be subdivided to avoid joint costs. The circumstances will vary, but, in essence, joint costs should be allocated as closely as possible to what is actually occurring in the project. Similar problems exist in allocating overhead. Often overhead is not included in labor, equipment, and material charges to the project; instead, it is treated as a single total cost for the activity or, more predominately, for the project.

The problems associated with activity-oriented cost systems can be formidable, but the benefits derived by overcoming the problems can be extensive. Although the cost segment of an integrated project information system is significant, time and resource control are also important. Major portions of the total information system can be examined by looking at the planning and scheduling phase and the implementing and controlling phase.

PLANNING AND SCHEDULING PHASE

From the previous chapters the reader should already have a good idea of the information needed for planning and scheduling. By using a form similar to the one shown in Figure 6-2, the project analyst or computer can

ACTIVITY		DEPARTMENT COST OR BUDGET ($)			
Number	Description	Engineering	Fabrication	Machining	Assembly

Figure 6-1 Organization/activity cost matrix

generate the traditional time, resource, and cost information for plans and schedules. Figure 6-3 presents the kind of information generated from the Input Data Form; this is a leveled time-constrained problem with the costs added. From the time-constrained schedule, Figure 6-4 shows the cumulative financial requirements for each period of the project. These cost figures were derived by assuming the cost expenditures for each activity are linear, that is, if the duration is 5 weeks and the total direct cost for the activity is $100,000, the weekly expenditure is $20,000. Activity 2-5, an exception, is inserted to make the point that activity costs may not be linear in practice. Of course, if resources or time are not constrained, the financial requirements could lie anywhere between the early and late start times. For example, if an early start schedule is used and the cash expenditures for any one period should be limited, one or more slack activities could be started later to delay cash expenditures. The resource schedule determined the financial budget for the example problem; see Figure 6-5. Note that the resource schedule, taken from Figure 6-4, lies between the early and late start schedules; the early and late financial requirements were computed using the format found in Figure 6-4.

When all the plans and schedules have been completed for labor, equipment, time, and cost, the stage is set for implementing and controlling the project.

IMPLEMENTING AND CONTROLLING PHASE

Once the project has started, the information system must be updated systematically so the current status of the project can be determined. This means collecting direct labor, equipment, and materials data. By collecting

| PROJECT TITLE | | | | | | | | | DEPARTMENT OR DIVISION | | DATE | | | PAGE ___ OF ___ |

The table (rotated 90°) contains the following labeled fields:

PROJECT TITLE — DEPARTMENT OR DIVISION — DATE — PAGE ___ OF ___

ACTIVITY DESCRIPTION

ESTIMATOR

APPROVED

DATE

LABOR AND/OR EQUIPMENT NEEDS / TIME PERIOD

SKILL AND/OR EQUIP-MENT		1	2	3	4	5	6	JOINT COSTS? LIST OTHER DEPARTMENTS
	H							
	$							
	H							
	$							
	H							
	$							
	H							

SKILL AND/OR EQUIPMENT

	H							
	$							
	H							
	$							
	H							
	$							
	H							
	$							

TOTAL LABOR HOURS _____
TOTAL MAN-DAYS _____
TOTAL EQUIPMENT HOURS _____

MATERIAL COST

MAJOR COMPONENTS	COST
1	
2	
3	
4	
5	
6	
7	
8	
9	
10 Miscl.	
TOTAL MATERIAL COST	$
TOTAL LABOR COST	$
TOTAL EQUIPMENT COST	$
ADDITIONAL JOINT COSTS TO THIS DEPT.	
TOTAL ACTIVITY COST	$
EXPECTED ACTIVITY DURATION	

ACTIVITY NO. ASSIGNED _____

H = Hours

Figure 6-2 Project input data form-time and direct cost estimates

Network Output Sheet

Act.	Dur.	Res.	ES	EF	LS	LF	TS	Cost
1-2	1	1	0	1	3	4	3	$ 3
1-3	2	2	0	2	0	2	0	4
1-4	3	2	0	3	4	7	4	15
2-5	4	1	1	5	4	8	3	24
3-5	6	0	2	8	2	8	0	30
3-6	3	2	2	5	7	10	5	6
4-6	3	2	3	6	7	10	4	9
5-7	4	1	8	12	8	12	0	16
6-7	2	2	6	8	10	12	4	4
								———
								$111

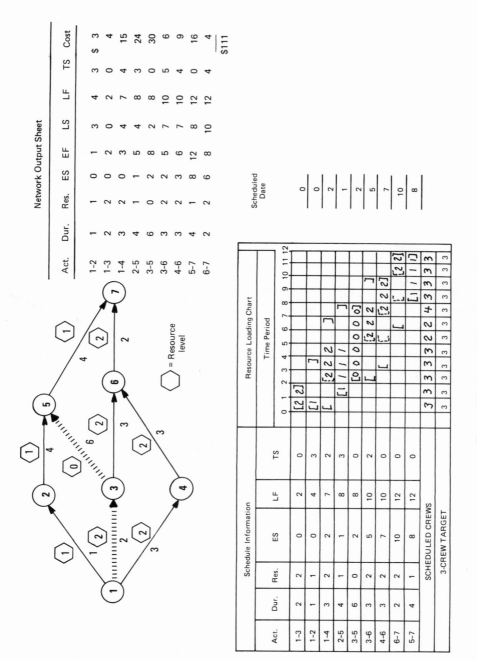

Schedule Information

Act.	Dur.	Res.	ES	LF	TS
1-3	2	2	0	2	0
1-2	1	1	0	4	3
1-4	3	2	2	7	2
2-5	4	1	1	8	3
3-5	6	0	2	8	0
3-6	3	2	5	10	2
4-6	3	2	7	10	0
6-7	2	2	10	12	0
5-7	4	1	8	12	0

Figure 6-3 A scheduled project with costs

Activity	Duration	Scheduled start	1	2	3	4	5	6	7	8	9	10	11	12	Activity cost budget
1-2	1	0	3												3
1-3	2	0	2	2											4
1-4	3	2			5	5	5								15
2-5	4	1		8	8	4	4								24
3-5	6	2			5	5	5	5	5	5					30
3-6	3	5						2	2	2					6
4-6	3	7								3	3	3			9
5-7	4	8									4	4	4	4	16
6-7	2	10											2	2	4
Total			5	10	18	14	14	7	7	10	7	7	6	6	111
Cumulative Total			5	15	33	47	61	68	75	85	92	99	105	111	

Figure 6-4 Financial requirements schedule and budget

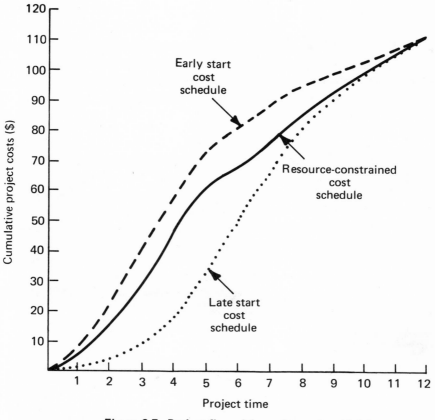

Figure 6-5 Project financial requirements schedules

the actual, planned, and latest revised estimates, the over/underruns in time and cost can be determined for each activity (work package) in the network and then for the project. For example, actual labor hours can be compared to planned labor hours. Any variance in actual can be converted to activity time and cost. The same procedure can be used on latest revised estimates of labor hours and the planned labor hours.

Cost Control

Since a great deal of the control effort centers around cost, let us use the example from the planning and scheduling phase to illustrate the cost side of the implementing and control phase. Figure 6-6 gives the actual costs to period 5, earned budget to period 5, and the latest revised cost estimates for the remainder of the project. The changes in cost that have taken place and those expected to take place are evident if the original cost budget is compared with the total-to-complete column. For example, the original budget for activity 3-5 is $30, but the revised estimate is $45; this represents a $15 cost overrun for the activity. There is a $26 (137 - 111) overrun for the project. Another valuable number shown in Figure 6-6 is the earned budget; this number represents the portion of the original budget that has been earned by the work actually performed to date; it is called "value of work completed" and "estimated cost to date." This earned budget is kept because it is possible that actual expenditures can keep up with the original budget, but the project could be several periods behind.

An explanation is needed of how the earned budget is computed. For activities already completed the original budget is recorded as the earned budget. There are two kinds of partially completed activities with which we must deal. First, there are in-process activities where the latest revised estimates are the same as those in the original budget; in these cases the earned budget up to the current period is the same as the original budget. Second, there are those in-process activities in which the latest revised estimates are not the same as the original budget; see activity 3-5 in Figure 6-6. In these cases, the value of the work performed to date must be allocated on the basis of the original budget. The following equation is used to compute the earned budget for an activity in process:

$$EB = OB \frac{AC}{RC}$$

where

EB = Earned budget
OB = Original budget (for activity)
AC = Actual cost (for period)
RC = Revised cost (for activity)

For example, to compute the earned budget for activity 3-5 in period 4, we would insert the following values in the equation:

$$EB = OB \left(\frac{AC}{RC}\right) = 30 \left(\frac{12}{45}\right) = 2 \left(\frac{12}{13}\right) = (2)(4) = 8$$

This reveals that although the actual expenditures were $12, the earned budget (based on the latest revised estimate) is only $8. Note that the earned budget can be computed for the cumulative value through period 5 where $EB = 30 (18/45) = 12. Since only about 10–15 percent of the activities are in process at any one time, the earned budget computations are not

ACTIVITY	DURATION	ORIG. COST BUDGET	ACTUAL COSTS REPORTED BY PERIOD (actual/earned)					ACTUAL COST TO DATE	LATEST REVISED COST ESTIMATES BY PERIOD									TOTAL TO COMPLETE
			1	2	3	4	5		6	7	8	9	10	11	12	13	14	
1-2	1	3	3/3					3										3
1-3	2	4	3/2	5/2				8										8
1-4	3	15		4/8	5/4	4/3		13										13
2-5	4	24			7/9	6/8	13/7	26										26
3-5	6	30				12/6	6/6	18	5	5	5	6	6					45
3-6	3	6							2	2	2							6
4-6	3	9									4	4	3					11
5-7	4	16												4	4	4	6	18
6-7	2	4														3	4	7
TOTAL ACTUAL		111	6	9	12	22	19	68	7	7	11	10	9	4	4	7	10	137
CUMULATIVE ACTUAL			6	15	27	49	68		75	82	93	103	112	116	120	127	137	
EARNED BUDGET			5	10	13	17	13											
CUMULATIVE EARNED BUDGET			5	15	28	45	58											

Legend: Actual / Earned

Figure 6-6 Current project cost status report

numerous. When updates are frequent, the cumulative procedure is some-times used; otherwise, if actual costs change each period, the earned budget for previous periods would have to be recalculated.

The information presented in the project cost status report is very use-ful for financial planning because it is presented by period. The same infor-mation can be rearranged for the whole project by activity. Figure 6-7 shows the project cost summary report, which directs attention to activity and project performance.

All of the data for the project are summarized in Figure 6-8, the project summary graph for the example problem. In a single glance the project man-ager can see several problems with this project. First, at the end of period 5 there is a $3 (61-58) cost overrun between earned budget and the original cost budget; plus, there is a $7 (68-61) cost overrun between actual and original cost budget. Assuming the latest revised estimates are reasonable, there will be a $26 cost overrun when the project is completed, and the project will be two periods late. Since the project was originally assumed to be time constrained, the project manager would have had a difficult time trying to cut costs and eliminate project time slippage simultaneously.

	Work Performed to Date			Total Cost at Completion		
Activity	Earned Budget Value	Actual Cost	Overrun Underrun	Original Cost Budget	Latest Revised Estimate	Overrun Underrun
1-2	3	3	0	3	3	0
1-3	4	8	(4)	4	8	(4)
1-4	15	13	(2)	15	13	2
2-5	24	26	(2)	24	26	(2)
3-5	12	18	(6)	30	45	(15)
3-6				6	6	0
4-6				9	11	(2)
5-7				16	18	(2)
6-7				4	7	(3)
Total	58	68	(10)	111	137	(26)

Figure 6-7 Project cost summary report

Time, Labor Hours, and Equipment Control.

Time, labor hours, and equipment control are very similar to cost control; that is, actual, planned, earned, and latest revised estimates for each activity are used to compute a summary graph similar to the one in Figure 6-8. Figure 6-9 shows another way of presenting the data for time and labor. Outlook reports designate trends that are developing. In this hypothetical project the schedule outlook report at time 55 indicates that the project is nine periods behind, but the trend is downward—from fifteen periods at time 40. When these reports are combined with the cost dimension, the project manager has a powerful tool. Outlook reports indicate quickly—for each dimension on which data are collected—where variances exist. Isolating important

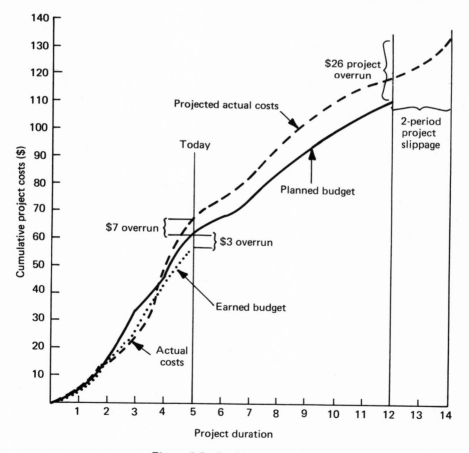

Figure 6-8 Project cost summary graph

control factors such as labor or time pinpoints problems more easily. Out-look reports are usually developed for the project; in large projects, how-ever, the same reports may be developed for organizations, departments, activities, or fragnets.

Problem and Corrective-Action Reports.

The reports described above do not pinpoint the *causes* of cost or time over-runs. Clearly, if the management by exception philosophy is to be used, some method is needed which will identify the causes of the problems and which will assure top management that steps have been taken to correct or stop adverse trends.

Figure 6-10 presents a problem and corrective action report form similar to those used in practice. This form is usually prepared by the first-line supervisor and reviewed by upper management. Essentially, this report asks the first-line supervisor what the problem is, what its influence is on the ac-tivity and project in terms of time and cost, and what action is required to solve the problem. If previous reports have been submitted, it is easy to see if solutions suggested earlier have been effective.

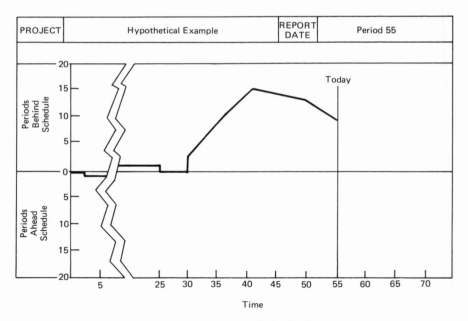

Figure 6-9 Time schedule outlook report

		Page ___ of ___
Project Title	Dept	Report Date
Activity Description		Activity Number
Early Start Date	Scheduled Start Date	Activity Duration
Actual Start	Slack Remaining Today	Previous Report Dates

Problem

Effect on Activity and Project

Time	Cost

Corrective Action Taken

_____
Signature

Figure 6-10 Problem and corrective action reports

MANUAL UPDATING OF TIME NETWORKS

A network that is not updated regularly loses its value quickly as conditions change. Many manual updating methods exist; most involve removing completed activities, recording actual start and completion times, estimating revised completion times, recording remaining slack, and identifying time over/underruns. Figure 6-11 exhibits the updated network of the example problem after period 5. Completed activities have zero activity times shown.

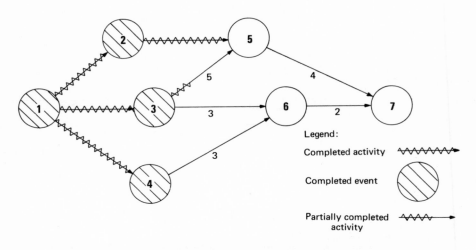

Figure 6-11   Updated network at time period 5

The network provides the following information. Activities 1-2, 1-3, 1-4, and 2-5 are completed as are events 1, 2, 3, and 4. Note that activity 3-5 is only partially completed. At the end of period 5, activity 3-5 has a duration of five periods left; this indicates that the project will be two time periods late, since activity 1-3 was one period late and 3-5 is going to be one period late.

In practice it is customary to accompany the updated network with a time progress table similar to the one shown in Figure 6-12. This table shows that activity 3-5 has been delayed because activity 1-3 took three time periods rather than the two planned, and the duration for activity 3-5 has been increased from six to seven periods. These two delays will cause the project to be two periods late. The information developed manually for this figure is very similar to output generated by computer programs. After considerable updating it may be advisable to redraw the network for the sake of clarity.

TRAINING

Successful application of PERT/CPM techniques in any organization requires that management at *all* levels have some degree of proficiency in their use. Training programs can do much to facilitate implementation and break down resistance to the use of the techniques when they are introduced. Since the degree of proficiency depends on the user, two types of training programs are recommended—one for top management and one for those who must implement the technique. Top management must have the ability to read and interpret the reports generated by the techniques.

Activity	Dur.	Scheduled Start	Scheduled Finish	Slack	Actual Start	Actual or Expected Finish	Remaining Slack	Act. Time Overrun/ Underrun
1-2	1	0	1	3	0	1	Finished	0
1-3	2	0	2	0	0	3	Finished	(1)
1-4	3	2	5	2	2	5	Finished	0
2-5	4	1	5	3	1	5	Finished	0
3-5	6	2	8	0	3	10	-2	
3-6	3	5	8	2		8	2	
4-6	3	7	10	0		10	0	
5-7	4	8	12	0		14	-2	
6-7	2	10	12	0		14	-2	

Figure 6-12 Time progress report at time period 5

Those who implement the techniques must collect the data, build the networks, assign accounting cost numbers, etc. Obviously, the latter group needs a thorough indoctrination in at least a three-to-five day training seminar and workshop which covers the equivalent of this text. The top-management group should cover similar material but with less emphasis on technique and more on understanding the total network-based system and how to use the information system for analysis.

If PERT/CPM systems have not been used before, outside consultants can set up an in-house training program to meet the needs of different groups within an organization. An in-house program is recommended because the total curriculum and selection of personnel can be better coordinated than one where employees are sent out to attend seminars by various organizations. The latter is suggested after the techniques have been used and most key people have been exposed to PERT/CPM systems.

QUESTIONS

6-1. What are the most common mistakes management has been known to make in implementing a project management system?

6-2. In a traditional product organization why would it be important for top management to spell out the authority and responsibilities of the project team?

6-3. Why should the level of network detail be no more than is absolutely necessary? Explain.

6-4. Define earned budget in your own words.

6-5. What kind of information would be found on the Problem And Corrective Action Reports?

EXERCISES

6-1. Given the network and cost information below, develop a Financial Requirements Schedule and Budget. Plot your budget on a graph. Assume costs are dispersed linearly.

ACTIVITY	DURATION	ES	LS	EF	LF	SLACK	BUDGET
1-2	5	0	7	5	12	7	$25
1-3	8	0	0	8	8	0	48
1-4	6	0	5	6	11	5	30
2-5	3	5	12	8	15	7	9
3-4	3	8	8	11	11	0	12
4-5	4	11	11	15	15	0	20

Assume the following information has been collected for you. Complete the Current Project Cost Status form on page 163. From your completed form, develop a Cost Summary Report and graph. What information would you offer at the next project management meeting?

6-2. A. Below is the standard computer output for a hypothetical project. (1) draw a project network and identify the critical activities. Then (2) develop a financial requirements schedule by period assuming an early start schedule and linearity of costs.

ACTIVITY	DURATION	ES	LS	EF	LF	TS	BUDGET
1-2	8	0	0	8	8	0	$ 480,000
1-4	10	0	0	10	10	0	400,000
1-5	2	0	12	2	14	12	140,000
2-5	6	8	8	14	14	0	300,000
2-6	7	8	10	15	17	2	210,000
4-5	4	10	10	14	14	0	280,000
4-6	5	10	12	15	17	2	400,000
5-6	3	14	14	17	17	0	270,000
							$2,480,000

CURRENT PROJECT COST STATUS REPORT

ACT	DUR	ORIG. BUD.	ACTUAL COSTS REPORTED BY PERIOD 1	2	3	4	5	ACTUAL TO DATE	LATEST REVISED COST ESTIMATES BY PERIOD 6	7	8	9	10	11	12	13	14	15	16	TOTAL TO COMPLETE
1-2	5	25	4	4	4	4	4	20	6	5	5									20
1-3	8	48	7	7	7	7	7	35	6	5	5									56
1-4	6	30	12	0	0	6		30	6											36
2-5	3	9							4	4	4									12
3-4	3	12										4	4	4	4					
4-5	4	20													5	5	5	5		
TOTAL ACTUAL			23	23				85												
CUM. ACTUAL			23	46																
EARNED BUD.																				
CUM. EARN. BUD.																				

Legend: Actual ⟋ Earned

B. The Current Project Cost Status Report is shown below (with some numbers missing). (1) Develop a Project Cost Summary Report and (2) graph for this project. (3) Given your completed reports, what conclusions can you draw concerning the current and future outlook for the project? How is this project doing? What advice could you offer the project manager?

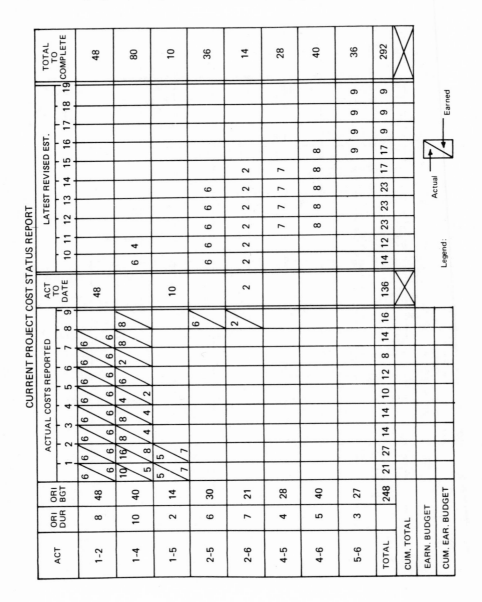

6-3. A staff specialist has provided you with the network information below.

1. Develop a Financial Requirements Schedule by period assuming costs are dispersed linearly. 2. The Current Project Cost Status Report is presented below. Work out a Cost Summary Report and graph. 3. Is the project completed on time? What is the critical path? Is there other information you have learned from these reports?

ACTIVITY	DURATION	BUDGET
1-2	4	$ 12
1-3	3	9
1-4	6	30
2-4	5	25
2-5	4	16
3-4	6	48
3-5	4	20
4-5	2	12
5-6	3	15
		$187

CURRENT PROJECT COST STATUS REPORT

ACT	ORG DUR	ORG BGT	ACTUAL COST REPORTED 1	2	3	4	5	6	ACTUAL TO DATE	LATEST REVISED COST ESTIMATES 7	8	9	10	11	12	13	14	15	TOTAL TO COMPLETE
1-2	4	12	4	4	4	4			16										16
1-3	3	9	3	3	3				9										9
1-4	6	30	7	7	7	7	7		35										35
2-4	5	25					5	5	10	5	5	5							25
2-5	4	16					8	4	12	2	2								16
3-4	6	48				9	9	9	27	9	9								
3-5	4	20				4	4	4	12	4									
4-5	2	12										6	6						
5-6	3	15												5	5	5			
TOTAL ACTUAL			14	14															
CUM ACTUAL			14	28															
EARNED BUDGET			12																
CUM EARN BGT																			

Legend: Actual — / Earned

PART IV
COMPUTER SYSTEMS

In this day and age it is difficult to think of employing project management techniques without the aid of a computer, even though it is possible to use the techniques manually. Application of the techniques presented in this text usually requires many trial runs in both the planning and scheduling phases of a project. The first plan is seldom the final plan. Things are left out of the plan, and usually many, "What if . . . " questions are considered before the final plan is accepted. Scheduling involves the same process for time and resources. Once the project is started the plan and schedule seldom occur as expected and more trial runs are needed to assess the new situation and circumstances. The advantages of the computer in doing this kind of work are obvious. With the development of reliable software programs for minicomputers, even managers with small projects can avoid some of the tedious detailed work required to enjoy the benefits of the techniques.

Purchasing, leasing, renting, or buying computer services can be costly if mistakes are made. Two extreme examples from the author's experience should illustrate. Both examples come from very large project organizations blessed with experienced project managers. The first organization wished to purchase a new software package which supposedly had more features than the one in current use and would make preparation of the input easier. As it turned out, neither the organization nor the software supplier noted that the organization was resource constrained, that is, the program assumed resources in each skill were unlimited. This made the program impossible to use. The company then purchased another program which was resource constrained from the software supplier. The cost of the first program was $22,000; the second program cost $17,000. The preparation of the input data proved far more difficult than for the program they had been using for years. Significant additional features were difficult to discern.

The second example is of an organization buying computer services for graphics. This organization showed the author two time-scaled networks drawn by the computer (they were beautiful and impressive). The project manager noted that the first one cost $500 and the second nearly $1,000. Since most projects in their organization require three to five years to complete, and since they update every month, the minimum cost for graphics alone on these two projects would be $54,000.

These examples point out two problems. The first organization did not understand or even try to assess what features they wanted from a computer program; the supplier sold them on the program package. Second, both organizations had little knowledge of the market. Similar programs and services could have been purchased at 25 percent of the price they paid. The lessons to be learned from these examples are simple. Know what you need before you shop; be sure to compare prices. The next chapter provides helpful guidelines for those who might be considering the use of computer-based **CPM** systems.

7
Computer-Based Project Management Information System

ANYONE engaged seriously in project management will eventually consider using a computer to assist in the planning, scheduling, and controlling processes. Ownership of a computer is not a prerequisite for considering use of one. If the project organization does not own or have access to a computer, it is possible to rent time from computer service bureaus found in most cities. Time sharing is available to almost any location that has a telephone. Time sharing uses a terminal and transmits PERT/CPM input data to a remote computer via telephone; the output is usually printed out on the user's terminal in printed or graphic form. For smaller firms or projects, use of teletypes is often adequate. Minicomputer companies are developing project management systems. Service bureaus and project consultants provide expert advice and will usually handle all of the details required for computer-based systems. This service can even include preparation of input data and interpretation of output reports.

Some background concerning the nature of computer-based PERT/CPM management information systems will be helpful to the uninitiated. The purpose of this chapter is to present an overview of the typical PERT/CPM information system and to show the format of the typical system output which management could expect in the early stages of the project.

The *raison d'être* of the PERT/CPM management information system is to provide management with timely and meaningful information for decision making. The computer-based systems available today have a record of providing dramatic improvements in the management of large, complex projects. Computer-based systems assist the manager in a very significant manner. Simply by using the system, the manager is provided with a *unified*

169

procedure to coordinate planning. Computer systems yield information for planning and evaluating alternative schedules. Once implementation of the project begins, the system assists the manager by furnishing information for measuring project progress. Most systems also allow the manager to test alternative strategies and assess their impact on the project. Clearly, as project size and complexity increase, so does the value of a computer-based PERT/CPM management information system.

DESCRIPTION OF A COMPUTER–BASED MANAGEMENT INFORMATION SYSTEM

A system is an on-going process composed of four major components—inputs, processor, outputs, and feedback. It is convenient to use these four terms to describe the PERT/CPM computer information system. Figure 7-1 presents the system in schematic form. Data inputs are gathered and fed into the computer which uses a computer program to calculate and manipulate the data to generate output reports for management. Management uses these reports to evaluate and make decisions. Management's response (feedback) is sent back to the system as input in the form of replanning and changes. Management replanning and changes along with progress data keep the information moving in a continuous cycle. The ability of the computer-based information system to handle large quantities of data quickly and accurately is invaluable.

INPUT AND OUTPUT REPORTS

The input component of the computer-based PERT/CPM information system essentially gathers data and prepares it for the computer. In the planning and scheduling stage data are gathered which identify and describe all the activities which must be completed before the project is finished. Next, information data are gathered which establish the dependencies of the activities in the project—predecessor and successor activities; the computer processes this information and develops the project network. Time data provide information for arrow diagrams, activity and event times, bar charts, and various sorts, such as slack or early start sorts. A calendar project start time and workday schedules allow the computer to compute completion dates and resource schedules. Cost data are gathered to develop budgets which will be used to compare actual progress with budgeted costs. A combination of time, cost, and resource data permits the computer to analyze and develop near optimal schedules for labor and equipment. Note that all these data are gathered *before* the project begins so tentative plans and schedules can be developed by the computer. Gathering this data is no small task, but the alternative of not gathering data is even less appealing.

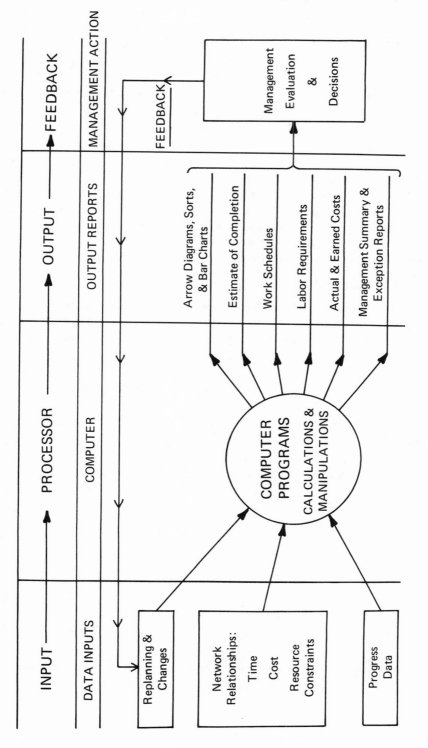

Figure 7-1   Computer-based PERT/CPM information system

Once tentative plans and schedules have been accepted and the project started, the main inputs are progress data and management replanning and changes. Actual completions are inputed and compared with time schedules to spot delays and possible bottlenecks. Labor availability and rescheduling are indicated—given the current status of the project. Actual costs are collected for all the resources used to complete the work packages. The system accepts new estimates of costs and completion dates. The computer program compares actual against budgets and schedules for management summary reports. The system allows management replanning and changes at any time during the life cycle of the project by accepting new input data and by generating a large variety of progress reports, summary reports, and "look ahead" reports. If, after extensive review, or at some point in the project, management wishes to simulate decisions relating to schedules or cost, the system will assess the impact of the alternative action.

COMPUTERS AND COMPUTER PROGRAMS

The processor in the management information system is the computer which follows a set of stored instructions to operate on input data and to print management reports. Virtually all of the major computer manufacturers have developed rather sophisticated computer-based PERT/CPM information systems (software). In general, the systems are similar in that each system provides planning, scheduling, and performance reports and accepts progress data and management changes. However, each software package of programs has its own scenarios in terms of capacity, restrictions, formats, capabilities, and special features such as random number assignment, multiple starts, graphic displays, conversion of standard networks to precedence networks, etc. Although changes occur continually in network-based systems, standards are beginning to emerge and most changes are only refinements of the basic system. Most refinements are occurring in resource allocation, cost, and graphics. In the final analysis the selection of a software package depends primarily on the needs of the user. Computer representatives, service bureaus, and/or consultants offer advice on programs, special features, and special problems.

WHEN IS A COMPUTER-BASED PERT/CPM MANAGEMENT INFORMATION SYSTEM NECESSARY?

An integrated management information system need not be a computer system. Manual systems work very well—up to a point. The dividing line between a manual and a computer management information system depends mainly on the user's needs and thus is different for each organization. Consideration of a computer system usually begins when management finds the manual system is inadequate in some sense—too slow, inaccurate, costly, impossible to get the desired information without a computer, etc. The decision has been made by hundreds of firms, and the factors they considered important have been recorded in the trade journals. The questions below represent a summary of those factors most frequently considered:

1. *How large is the project network?* Any size project can be handled effectively by a computer management information system. Thus, on smaller projects the manager has the option—manual or computer. When projects pass the 200–300 activity mark, however, the ability of the computer to do the network calculations, manipulations, updating, and analysis quickly and accurately usually surpasses manual methods.

2. *How frequently will reports be required?* This is often the point where manual methods break down. If frequent reports are a requirement, manual reporting systems can quickly become inundated with paper work. For example, if one or two activities in the project become delayed, it may require several thousand calculations to revise networks, schedules, and management reports. The computer can handle these changes in a matter of minutes, whereas manual methods may require days. Generally, updating and reports take place biweekly or once a month.

3. *How complex is the network and how important is coordination?* Complex projects usually present serious problems of coordination. Coordination is a problem in complex networks where many diverse groups are working independently but their tasks are highly dependent on each other, e.g., subcontractors. Computer-based PERT/CPM information systems assist management by providing everyone with the same output and by identifying those who are on the critical path; everyone knows the status of the other groups. Since everyone receives the same output, communication is facilitated.

4. *What is the duration of the project?* Setting up the information system for a project incurs a considerable amount of time. The project may be too short to enjoy the benefits of the computer-based information system. Also, the status reports may not be timely enough to do any good if activities and the project are of short duration.

5. *What features are required for the management information system?* If only network time information is required, perhaps manual methods are adequate. If time, cost, and labor schedules are expected, a computer may be imperative. In general, it is safe to say that, as the number of features needed increases, so does the need for electronic assistance. For example,

resource leveling often requires several hundred iterations to get a nearoptimal answer. Addition of only the cost feature may increase the computations more than threefold.

Being limited to a selected computer may restrict the user to the features available in the software package that goes with that computer. Transportability of computer programs from one computer manufacturer to another is also limited. Hence, if the available system does not possess the necessary features, users may have to go outside to another computer or to design and program their own features. The costs of outside service and/or programming should be compared with the benefits.

6. *What is the total dollar value of the project?* The larger the dollar value of the project, the greater the cost of being wrong. Hence the planning and controlling of time, cost, labor, materials, and money become more important as the dollar value of the project gets larger. Computers can do a great deal to facilitate control through status reports, management reports, and analysis of alternative courses of action. In projects of small total dollar value, the benefits of the computer management information system may not be significant.

7. *Is a computer available or must time be rented?* If the computer is owned and on location, present equipment may be adequate. Since the cost of the computer is already sunk, the out-of-pocket costs may be only the direct costs of storage, input costs, and the one-time cost of training. Of course, this assumes that excess capacity exists, the computer is large enough, and a program is available. Leasing on location is similar to owning on location, except that the lease may specify the number of hours of operation per day; if the time is filled with other work, the additional PERT/CPM information system would add to the cost directly.

Renting computer time off location can sometimes present problems, but not necessarily. Simply the geographical distance of off-location computers can create problems at times. Firms often rent their computers during off hours (e.g., 6 P.M. to midnight), but this is not always convenient for the project user. Also, renters often have last priority if breakdowns occur. Time sharing is a good alternative for small businesses, even though the input-output devices are often slow, for example, use of a teletype terminal; in small businesses this may not be a critical factor.

8. *Will the system be used continually or only for one project?* If the system is to be used on more than one project, the setup costs can be distributed. On the other hand, a single project may be so large and complex that a computer is a necessity. Employing consultants who are specialists in PERT/CPM is often the best route if the personnel of the firm are not

familiar with the computer system. If possible, though, management prefers to spread the setup costs over several projects.

9. *Are experienced computer personnel available or will training be required?* The time and cost of training can be significant factors in the introduction of a management information system. In some cases the features of the system which management desires require special programming which in turn requires some knowledge of PERT/CPM techniques.

Small firms with little PERT/CPM experience would be well advised to work gradually into the computer-based PERT/CPM information system if possible. For example, they could use a computer system on a trial project, employing only the time-scheduling features. This system usually provides planning networks, activity and event times, bar charts, completion dates, status reports, and look-ahead management reports. The costs of such a system are minimal, and the experience gained is useful in assessing the value of adding cost and resource allocation features to the system for other projects.

The question of when to use the computer deserves careful study because mistakes in either direction can be costly. In the final analysis the question of when to use a computer-based information system is a matter of comparing the costs versus the benefits—both explicit and implicit. The value of information is difficult to measure, but such intangibles must be given serious consideration; for example, how effective is the present system in facilitating management control versus the proposed computer-based system? If the decision is made to go with a computer-based PERT/CPM information system, support of top management is a must.

EXAMPLES OF COMPUTER OUTPUTS

Some typical computer outputs are presented in Figure 7-2. The figure shows the computer output for the construction of a yacht to be used in races. Part (a) is the input data provided by the project manager. The i is the start event number for an activity and the j is the finish event number for an activity. Part (b) presents a typical computer output for the construction of the yacht. The early, late, and slack times for each activity are given; the critical activities are labeled. Part (c) presents a Gantt chart of the project. The chart is on a time scale. Note that the critical activities have no slack and the duration is 24 weeks. Free slack is a special form of total slack; it is sometimes important because an activity with free slack can be delayed for the slack time without rescheduling any activities following it.

The computer forms and outputs found in figures 7-3 to 7-8 represent a simple, hypothetical, multiproject, multiskill, resource-constrained forest organization similar to some districts of the United States Forest Service. The three projects are identical in all aspects except for their starting times.

(a)

INPUT DATA LIST

YACHT PROJECT

I	J	DURATION	ACTIVITY DESCRIPTION
1	2	2	DESIGN AND BLUEPRINTS
2	3	8	BUILD ALUMINUM HULL
2	4	8	ORDER MAST AND FITTINGS
2	5	11	ORDER DECK FITTINGS
3	5	6	BUILD DECK
3	6	4	PAINT HULL
4	6	9	ORDER AND MAKE SAILS
5	6	7	INSTALL DECK FITTINGS
-6	7	1	INSTALL MAST AND RIGGING

(b)

PROJECT ACTIVITY TIMES

YACHT PROJECT

I	J	DURATION	ES	LS	EF	LF	TS	
1	2	2	0	0	2	2	0	CRITICAL
2	3	8	2	2	10	10	0	CRITICAL
2	4	8	2	6	10	14	4	
2	5	11	2	5	13	16	3	
3	5	6	10	10	16	16	0	CRITICAL
3	6	4	10	19	14	23	9	
4	6	9	10	14	19	23	4	
5	6	7	16	16	23	23	0	CRITICAL
-6	7	1	23	23	24	24	0	CRITICAL

(c)
BAR TIME CHART

YACHT PROJECT

I	J	DURATION	ACTIVITY DESCRIPTION	WEEK 01234567890	20
1	2	2	DESIGN AND BLUEPRINTS	xx	
2	3	8	BUILD ALUMINUM HULL	xxxxxxxx	
2	4	8	ORDER MAST AND RIGGING	xxxxxxxx0000	
2	5	11	ORDER DECK FITTINGS	xxxxxxxxxxx***	
3	5	6	BUILD DECK	xxxxxx	
3	6	4	PAINT HULL	xxxx**********	
4	6	9	ORDER AND MAKE SAILS	xxxxxxxxx****	
5	6	7	INSTALL DECK FITTINGS	xxxxxxx	
-6	7	1	INSTALL MAST AND RIGGING	x	

SYMBOL LEGEND:
x = Job week when work is being done or waiting

* = Activity free slack is the maximum time an activity can be delayed without delaying other successor activities linked to it

0 = Amount of time an activity can be delayed without delaying the finish time of the project

Figure 7-2 Sample computer network input data

Figure 7-3 shows the first input sheet that must be filled in to have the computer schedule activities and resources. Since all projects do not usually start on the same day, the three projects found in this example—activities 2-110, 2-235, and 2-360—are started on workdays 0, 30, and 60, respectively. Activity 2-6998 defines the planning period, which in this case is 185 days. The information below this point identifies the project, activity, duration, crafts and quantity required, and description. For example, the information for activity 112-114 would be interpreted as follows: the activity is a part of project 10, the activity number is 112-114, the duration is two workdays, one unit of skill 78 is required and one unit of skill 79 is required, and the job description is OTHER RES. INPUT. From the top of the page it is evident that this is only one of twelve pages of input required for the three projects.

Figure 7-4 shows the input required to schedule the different crafts. In the simplified example only 19 crafts are used and it is assumed only one unit of each craft is available. The cost and days available have been omitted for simplicity.

Given the above inputs and some additional inputs, the computer sets up a multiproject and multiskill plan, and resource schedule. Figure 7-5 presents the multiproject plan assuming *unlimited* resources. Project 1 is given an item number of 10, project 2, 20, and project 3, 30.

Since the multiproject network was set up to be limited to 185 work-days, all float was computed using this constraint. In this case the 185 days were used so the critical path would have zero float; normally this figure might represent the end of the planning period, e.g., one year, five years, or be the time for the project with the longest duration. Project 1 would be completed in 125 workdays if resources are unlimited. Project 2 would be completed by day 155 and project 3 by day 185 if resources are unlimited.

Figure 7-6 gives a single page of the schedule of resources. Observe that both the calendar date and workday are provided; the workday can be used to cross-reference with several other output reports. Project 2 starts on workday 30 and, of course, competes for resources by the heuristics found in this program. By day 37, activity 119-122 is delayed two days because skill 10 is being used on activity 237-240; see day 32—skill 10 is going to be used for five days (32+5=37) which means it will not be available for activity 119-122 on day 35; thus this activity has two days' negative float.

Other output available to the project manager is a summary schedule for any particular resource, be it labor or equipment. Figure 7-7 presents a workday schedule for the RECON. FRSTR. which is resource craft 14. The negative float may be caused by the limitation of several resources—not just resource number 14.

Note that workdays can be changed to calendar dates by looking at output in Figure 7-6. This information is very useful to the project manager for scheduling this resource; of course, under normal conditions this resource is scheduled for more than 95 workdays.

Most multiproject programs provide a summary schedule for each project. Figure 7-8 shows the schedule for project 3. Recall that in our plan we expected all the projects to be completed by day 185. However, *given the resource constraints* and the program scheduling heuristics, Projects 1, 2, and 3 cannot be completed as planned by days 125, 155 and 185, respectively. In this example they can be completed by days 127, 182, and 217, respectively; the latter is shown in Figure 7-8 at the bottom of the column labeled Sched. Finish. The 32 days of negative float is the 185-217 =-32. Such summary schedules are very useful if different projects have different managers responsible for each one.

USDA – FOREST SERVICE

FOREST		DATE
DIVISION		BY

CPMS NETWORK DATA

CPMS SELL PROJECT DATA

PAGE 1 OF 12

ITEM NUMBER	NODES START FINISH I	NODES J	DURATION	RESOURCE REQUIREMENTS CRAFT NUMBER – NUMBER REQ'D				FUND	ESTIMATED FIXED COST	JOB DESCRIPTION (26 LETTERS AND SPACES)	ROAD NUMBER
XXX	XXXX	XXXX	XXXX	X X X	XX XX	XX XX	XX X	XXXXX	XX	26 LETTERS AND SPACES	XXX XXX
000	0001	0002								LEAD	XXX XXX
000	0002	0110								START PROJECT 1	
000	0002	0235	0030							START PROJECT 2	
000	0002	0360	0060 0							START PROJECT 3	
000	0002	6998	0185 0							NETWORK RESTRAINT 185 DAYS	
010	0110	0111	1	10 1						OFFICE RECON	
010	0110	0112	1	11 1						PREL FIELD RECON	
010	0112	0113	2	85 1						TH SO INPUT	
010	0112	0114	2	78 1	79 1					OTHER RES INPUT	
010	0112	0115	5	12 1						EAR PREP	
010	0113	0115								PSEUDO	
010	0114	0115								PSEUDO	
010	0115	0116	20							EAR REVIEW	
010	0116	0117	1	21 1						LOC ENGR R2	
010	0116	0118	1	21 1						LOC ENGR R1	

Figure 7-3 Sample computer network input data

USDA – FOREST SERVICE

FOREST			DATE		CPMS RESOURCE DATA	
DIVISION			BY			

CPMS   SELL PROJECT DATA   PAGE 10 OF 12

Code 1	Craft Number 3	Units Available 6	RATE $ PER DAY 9		DAY AVAILABLE 13	POSITION 17
XX	XX	XXX	XX	XX	XXXX	24 LETTERS AND SPACES
03	10	1				*FRSTRY AIDE*
03	11	1				*PRE SALE CREW*
03	12	1				*ORF DIST STAFF*
03	14	1				*RECON FRSTR*
03	20	1				*ENGR SURVEY CREW 1*
03	21	1				*ENGR SURVEY CREW 2*
03	22	1				*FRST SURVEY CREW 1*
03	26	1				*FRST SURVEY CREW 2*
03	40	1				*DIST COORD STAFF*
03	50	1				*TMBR STAFF*
03	78	1				*LANDSCAPE ARCHITECT*
03	79	1				*ROW STAFF ASST*
03	85	1				*SILVI CULTURIST*
03	87	1				*RESRCE CLK 1*
03	89	1				*RESRCE CLK 2*
03	90	1				*FRST ENGR*
03	91	1				*PRE CONST ENGR*
03	93	1				*DESIGNERS SO*
03	94	1				*SO SURVEY PRTY CHF*
03	99	999				
03						
03						
03						
-3	99	999				MISC. ← *LAST CARD*

Figure 7-4   Sample computer input for skills available

NETWORK DATA AND CRITICAL PATH

ITEM NO.	I NODE	J NODE	DURATION	RESOURCE REQUIREMENTS I	II	III	IV	FUND	FIXED COST	JOB DESCRIPTION	EARLY START	LATE START	EARLY FINISH	LATE FINISH	FLOAT
000	2	235	30					-0	-0	START PROJECT 2	0	0	30	30	0
000	2	368	60					-0	-0	START PROJECT 3	0	0	60	60	0
000	2	6998	185					-0	-0	NETWORK RESTRAINT 185 DAYS	0	0	185	185	0
010	110	111	1	10-1				-0	-0	OFFICE RECON	0	0	1	1	0
010	111	112	1	11-1				-0	-0	PREL FIELD RECON	1	1	2	2	0
010	112	113	2	85-1				-0	-0	TM SO INPUT	2	5	4	7	3
010	112	114	2	78-1	79-1			-0	-0	OTHER RES INPUT	2	5	4	7	3
010	112	115	5	12-1				-0	-0	EAR PREP	2	2	7	7	0
010	115	116	20					-0	-0	EAR REVIEW	7	7	27	27	0
010	116	117	1	21-1				-0	-0	LOC ENGR R2	27	34	28	35	7
010	116	118	1	21-1				-0	-0	LOC ENGR R1	27	34	28	35	7
010	116	119	8	12-1				-0	-0	TM RECON	27	27	35	35	0
010	117	120	2	22-1	26-1			-0	-0	SURVEY	28	60	30	62	32
010	118	121	4	22-1	26-1			-0	-0	SURVEY	28	50	32	54	22
010	119	122	2	10-1	40-1			-0	-0	DIST COORD REVIEW	35	35	37	37	0
010	120	123	8	93-1	94-1			-0	-0	DESIGN	30	62	38	70	32
010	121	124	15	93-1	94-1			-0	-0	DESIGN	32	54	47	69	22
010	122	125	10	12-1	14-1			-0	-0	SALE LAYOUT	37	37	47	47	0
010	123	126	1	20-1	91-1			-0	-0	PLAN IN HAND	38	70	39	71	32
010	124	127	1	20-1	91-1			-0	-0	PLAN IN HAND	47	69	48	70	22
010	125	128	15	12-1	14-1			-0	-0	CRUISE OR MARK	47	47	62	62	0
010	126	129	1	91-1				-0	-0	COST EST	39	71	40	72	32
010	127	129	2	91-1				-0	-0	COST EST	48	70	50	72	22
010	128	129	10					-0	-0	ADP RO	62	62	72	72	0
010	129	130	6	50-1				-0	-0	SALE CONTR	72	76	78	82	4
010	129	131	10	14-1				-0	-0	APPRAISE	72	72	82	82	0
010	131	132	20	87-1				-0	-0	SO TM REVIEW	82	82	102	102	0
010	132	133	2	89-1	90-1			-0	-0	AD PREP	102	102	104	104	0
010	133	134	20					-0	-0	AD	104	104	124	124	0
010	134	135	1	10-1	11-1			-0	-0	SELL	124	124	125	125	0
000	135	6998	60					-0	-0	PROJECT 1 COMPLETED	125	125	185	185	0
020	235	236	1	10-1				-0	-0	OFFICE RECON	30	30	31	31	0
020	236	237	1	14-1				-0	-0	PREL FIELD RECON	31	31	32	32	0
020	237	238	2	85-1				-0	-0	TM SO INPUT	32	35	34	37	3
020	237	239	2	78-1	79-1			-0	-0	OTHER RES INPUT	32	35	34	37	3
020	237	240	5	10-1				-0	-0	EAR PREP	32	32	37	37	0
020	240	241	20					-0	-0	EAR REVIEW	37	37	57	57	0
020	241	242	1	20-1				-0	-0	LOC ENGR R2	57	64	58	65	7
020	241	243	1	20-1				-0	-0	LOC ENGR R1	57	64	58	65	7
020	241	244	8	14-1				-0	-0	TM RECON	57	57	65	65	0
020	242	245	2	22-1	26-1			-0	-0	SURVEY	58	90	60	92	32
020	243	246	4	22-1	26-1			-0	-0	SURVEY	58	80	62	84	22
020	244	247	2	10-1	40-1			-0	-0	DIST COORD REVIEW	65	65	67	67	0
020	245	248	8	93-1	94-1			-0	-0	DESIGN	60	92	68	100	32
020	246	249	15	93-1	94-1			-0	-0	DESIGN	62	84	77	99	22
020	247	250	10	12-1	14-1			-0	-0	SALE LAYOUT	67	67	77	77	0
020	248	251	1	20-1	91-1			-0	-0	PLAN IN HAND	68	100	69	101	32
020	249	252	1	20-1	91-1			-0	-0	PLAN IN HAND	77	99	78	100	22
020	250	253	15	12-1	14-1			-0	-0	CRUISE OR MARK	77	77	92	92	0
020	251	254	1	91-1				-0	-0	COST EST	69	101	70	102	32
020	252	254	2	91-1				-0	-0	COST EST	78	100	80	102	22
020	253	254	10					-0	-0	ADP RO	92	92	102	102	0
020	254	255	6	50-1				-0	-0	SALE CONTR	102	106	108	112	4
020	254	256	10	12-1				-0	-0	APPRAISE	102	102	112	112	0
020	256	257	20	87-1				-0	-0	SO TM REVIEW	112	112	132	132	0
020	257	258	2	89-1	90-1			-0	-0	AD PREP	132	132	134	134	0
020	258	259	20					-0	-0	AD	134	134	154	154	0
020	259	260	1	11-1	12-1			-0	-0	SELL	154	154	155	155	0
000	260	6998	30					-0	-0	PROJECT 2 COMPLETED	155	155	185	185	0
030	360	361	1	10-1				-0	-0	OFFICE RECON	60	60	61	61	0
030	361	362	1	14-1				-0	-0	PREL FIELD RECON	61	61	62	62	0
030	362	363	2	85-1				-0	-0	TM SO INPUT	62	65	64	67	3
030	362	364	2	78-1	79-1			-0	-0	OTHER RES INPUT	62	65	64	67	3
030	362	365	5	12-1				-0	-0	EAR PREP	62	62	67	67	0
030	365	366	20					-0	-0	EAR REVIEW	67	67	87	87	0
030	366	367	1	20-1				-0	-0	LOC ENGR R2	87	94	88	95	7
030	366	368	1	20-1				-0	-0	LOC ENGR R1	87	94	88	95	7
030	366	369	8	12-1				-0	-0	TM RECON	87	87	95	95	0
030	367	370	2	22-1	26-1			-0	-0	SURVEY	88	120	90	122	32
030	368	371	4	22-1	26-1			-0	-0	SURVEY	88	110	92	114	22
030	369	372	2	10-1	40-1			-0	-0	DIST COORD REVIEW	95	95	97	97	0
030	370	373	8	93-1	94-1			-0	-0	DESIGN	90	122	98	130	32
030	371	374	15	93-1	94-1			-0	-0	DESIGN	92	114	107	129	22
030	372	375	10	12-1	14-1			-0	-0	SALE LAYOUT	97	97	107	107	0
030	373	376	1	20-1	91-1			-0	-0	PLAN IN HAND	98	130	99	131	32
030	374	377	1	20-1	91-1			-0	-0	PLAN IN HAND	107	129	108	130	22
030	375	378	15	12-1	14-1			-0	-0	CRUISE OR MARK	107	107	122	122	0
030	376	379	1	91-1				-0	-0	COST EST	99	131	100	132	32
030	377	379	2	91-1				-0	-0	COST EST	108	130	110	132	22
030	378	379	10					-0	-0	ADP RO	122	122	132	132	0
030	379	380	6	50-1				-0	-0	SALE CONTR	132	136	138	142	4
030	379	381	10	12-1				-0	-0	APPRAISE	132	132	142	142	0
030	381	382	20	87-1				-0	-0	SO TM REVIEW	142	142	162	162	0
030	382	383	2	89-1	90-1			-0	-0	AD PREP	162	162	164	164	0
030	383	384	20					-0	-0	AD	164	164	184	184	0
030	384	385	1	10-1	11-1			-0	-0	SELL	184	184	185	185	0

Figure 7-5   Mulitproject plan

CPMS SFLL PROJECT DATA
CRAFT GROUP SUMMARY
JUNE 10

RECON　FRSTR

ITEM NO.	SCHD. START	DURA TION	SCHD. FINISH	LATE START	JOB FLOAT	JOB DESCRIPTION	I NODE	J NODE	I	II	III	IV	FUND	CHAR
020	31	1	32	31	–	PREL FIELD RECON	236	237	14- 1					
010	39	10	49	37	-2	SALF LAYOUT	122	125	12- 1	14- 1				
010	49	15	64	47	-2	CRUISE OR MARK	125	128	12- 1	14- 1				
020	64	8	72	57	-7	TM RECON	241	244	14- 1					
030	72	1	73	61	-11	PREL FIELD RECON	361	362	14- 1					
010	74	10	84	72	-2	APPRAISE	129	131	14- 1					
020	84	10	94	67	-17	SALE LAYOUT	247	250	12- 1	14- 1				
020	94	15	109	77	-17	CRUISE OR MARK	250	253	12- 1	14- 1				
030	119	10	129	97	-22	SALE LAYOUT	372	375	12- 1	14- 1				
030	139	15	154	107	-32	CRUISE OR MARK	375	378	12- 1	14- 1				

Figure 7-6　Multiproject schedule

CPMS SELL PROJECT DATA
MANSCHEDULE REPORT

JUNE 10

ITEM NO.	WORK DAY	JOB STATUS	JOB DESCRIPTION	I NODE	J NODE	DURA TION	FLOAT	I	II	III	IV	FUND	CHARGE
010	29	FINISH	LOG ENGR R1	116	118	1	6						
	FEB 13												
000	30	FINISH	START PROJECT 2	2	235	30	0						
010	30	FINISH	SURVEY	117	120	2	32						
020	30	START	OFFICE RECON	235	236	1	0	10- 1				0	0
010	30	START	SURVEY	118	121	4	20	22- 1	26- 1			0	0
010	30	START	DESIGN	120	123	8	32	93- 1	94- 1			0	0
	FEB 16												
020	31	FINISH	OFFICE RECON	235	236	1	0						
020	31	START	PREL FIELD RECON	236	237	1	0	14- 1				0	0
	FEB 17												
020	32	FINISH	PREL FIELD RECON	236	237	1	0						
020	32	START	EAR PREP	237	240	5	0	10- 1				0	0
020	32	START	TM SO INPUT	237	238	2	3	85- 1				0	0
020	32	START	OTHER RES INPUT	237	239	2	3	78- 1	79- 1			0	0
	FEB 18												
	FEB 19												
010	34	FINISH	SURVEY	118	121	4	20						
020	34	FINISH	TM SO INPUT	237	238	2	3						
020	34	FINISH	OTHER RES INPUT	237	239	2	3						
	FEB 20												
010	35	FINISH	TM RECON	116	119	8	0						
	FEB 24												
	FEB 25												
020	37	FINISH	EAR PREP	237	230	5	0						
010	37	START	DIST COORD REVIEW	119	122	2	-2	10- 1	40- 1			0	0
020	37	START	EAR REVIEW	240	241	20	0					0	0
	FEB 26												
010	38	FINISH	DESIGN	120	123	8	32						
010	38	START	DESIGN	121	124	15	16	93- 1	94- 1			0	0
010	38	START	PLAN IN HAND	123	126	1	32	20- 1	91- 1			0	0
	FEB 27												
010	39	FINISH	DIST COORD REVIEW	119	122	2	-2						
010	39	FINISH	PLAN IN HAND	123	126	1	32						
010	39	START	SALE LAYOUT	122	125	10	-2	12- 1	14- 1			0	0
010	39	START	COST EST	126	129	1	32	91- 1				0	0
	MAR 1												
010	40	FINISH	COST EST	126	129	1	32						
	MAR 2												
	MAR 3												
	MAR 4												
	MAR 5												
	MAR 8												
	MAR 9												
	MAR 10												
	MAR 11												
	MAR 12												
010	49	FINISH	SALE LAYOUT	122	125	10	-2						
010	49	START	CRUISE OR MARK	125	128	15	-2	12- 1	14- 1			0	0
	MAR 15												

Figure 7-7　Craft summary schedule

CPMS SELL PROJECT DATA
PROJECT GROUP SUMMARY
JUNE 10

ITEM NO.	SCHD. START	DURA TION	SCHD. FINISH	LATE START	JOB FLOAT	JOB DESCRIPTION	I NODE	J NODE	RESOURCE REQUIREMENTS				FUND	CHARGE
									I	II	III	IV		
030	60	1	61	60	8	OFFICE RECON	360	361	10- 1				0	0
030	72	1	73	61	-11	PRFL FIELD RECON	361	362	14- 1				0	0
030	73	5	78	62	-11	EAR PREP	362	365	12- 1				0	0
030	73	2	75	65	-8	TM SO INPUT	362	363	85- 1				0	0
030	73	2	75	65	-8	OTHER RES INPUT	362	364	78- 1	79- 1			0	0
030	78	20	98	57	-11	EAR REVIEW	365	366					0	0
030	98	1	99	94	-4	LOC ENGR R2	366	367	20- 1				0	0
030	99	1	100	94	-5	LOC ENGR R1	366	368	20- 1				0	0
030	99	2	101	120	21	SURVEY	367	370	22- 1	26- 1			0	0
030	101	4	105	110	9	SURVEY	368	371	22- 1	26- 1			0	0
030	101	8	109	122	21	DESIGN	370	373	93- 1	94- 1			0	0
030	109	8	117	87	-22	PLAN IN HAND	366	369	12- 1				0	0
030	109	15	124	114	5	COST EST	371	374	93- 1	94- 1			0	0
030	109	1	110	130	21	DIST COORD REVIEW	373	376	20- 1	91- 1			0	0
030	110	1	111	131	21	COST EST	376	379	91- 1				0	0
030	117	2	119	95	-22	DIST COORD REVIEW	369	372	10- 1	40- 1			0	0
030	119	10	129	97	-22	SALE LAYOUT	372	375	12- 1	14- 1			0	0
030	124	1	125	129	5	PLAN IN HAND	374	377	20- 1	91- 1			0	0
030	125	1	127	130	5	COST EST	377	379	91- 1				0	0
030	139	15	154	107	-32	CRUISE OR MARK	375	378	12- 1	14- 1			0	0
030	154	10	164	122	-32	ADP RO	378	379					0	0
030	164	10	174	132	-32	APPRAISE	379	381	12- 1				0	0
030	164	6	170	136	-28	SALE CONTR	379	380	50- 1				0	0
030	174	20	194	142	-32	SO TM REVIEW	381	382	87- 1				0	0
030	194	2	196	162	-32	AD PREP	382	383	89- 1	90- 1			0	0
030	196	20	216	164	-32	AD	383	384					0	0
030	216	1	217	184	-32	SELL	384	385	10- 1	11- 1			0	0

Figure 7-8   Project 3 schedule

QUESTIONS

7-1. What factors must be considered when deciding if a computer PERT/CPM information system should be used?

7-2. When would it be advisable to use outside consultants?

PART V
DEALING WITH
UNCERTAINTY

All of the methods described to this point assume that what is planned and scheduled will occur with certainty. Anyone who has been a manager more than a week knows that plans and schedules rarely work out in all aspects. Things that cannot be predicted always occur at what seems to be the wrong time and place. This part presents two approaches which recognize the uncertainty of activity time estimates and attempt to utilize better the information available to the project manager. Both approaches are used primarily as planning tools and are usually used before the project begins or sometimes midway when replanning is necessary. Chapter 8 discusses the PERT technique (Program Evaluation Review Technique) which is almost identical to the CPM technique discussed in chapters 2 and 3 with the exception that PERT uses three time estimates for each activity to compute the chances of completing an event successfully by a particular date. More specifically, PERT provides a procedure for quantitatively expressing the uncertainty associated with a completion date. It assumes the time estimate of an activity lies within the range of an optimistic and a pessimistic time (for example, 10 and 20 weeks). Chapter 9 presents PERT simulation—a technique which utilizes the same input information developed for PERT to simulate almost all the possible combinations of activity and project durations that can occur. PERT simulation copes with the *dynamics* of a project before the project is started.

Over the years the popularity of PERT has diminished with most users switching to the critical path methods presented earlier. With hindsight the demise of the PERT approach could have been predicted. Stated frankly, PERT requires the collection of three time estimates, which are often difficult and costly to get, and PERT requires a significant amount of computation for the ability to predict the probability of completing the project or an event successfully by a scheduled deadline. Managers recognized that the cost of collecting and manipulating the data often exeeded the benefits

185

of the information generated. The reader may be skeptical at this point and feel the marginal return of continuing is more academic than practical. This may not be the case. If PERT and PERT simulation are used together the benefits of the additional information that accrue to the project manager may be significant indeed.

Project managers frequently avoid even attempting to deal with uncertainty on the basis that their time estimates are not accurate. To do this with time estimates suggests a preference to use only estimated average times even though the manager may have a reasonable "feel" for the degree of reliability of the time estimate—e.g., plus or minus 10 percent. To ignore this additional information and make decisions on the basis of only limited and selected information is analogous to saying that guessing is better than an educated guess. To not use all the information available defies our rational instincts.

As more and more people use network techniques to manage projects, it seems inevitable that there will be a resurgence of PERT used in conjection with PERT simulation. Whether or not PERT or PERT simulation is used depends primarily on the cost or importance of being wrong. If the uncertainty of time estimates is relatively small and unimportant, PERT and PERT simulation offer little. If the critical path is clearly dominant and there are no "near-critical" paths that have small slack values, the benefits of PERT and PERT simulation may not be significant. However, if there is a reasonable possibility of shifting critical paths and if identifying possible critical activities and possible bottlenecks *before* the project begins is important, the combination of PERT and PERT simulation can provide valuable information for the project manager.

8
PERT

THE PERT (*p*rogram *e*valuation *r*eview *t*echnique) technique was developed for the Special Projects Office of the Navy to schedule and coordinate over 3,000 subcontractors and agencies working on the Polaris missile system used on submarines. PERT attempts to deal with some of the problems of uncertainty inherent in nonstandard and new technology projects. All the principles and methods explained in chapters 2 and 3 are applicable to the PERT technique, that is, the critical path, slack, and early and late times are all computed exactly as described. A thorough understanding of these chapters will be assumed.

OVERVIEW

The PERT developers wanted to have some way of recognizing and coping with variability in activity and project time estimates. For example, a contractor who gives a project time estimate of twelve weeks for building and erecting a ski lift on a mountain knows that the chances of completing the task in exactly twelve weeks are slim. With ideal conditions, such as weather, rock formation, and supplies, the chances of finishing early are good. Conversely, if these are not as anticipated, chances are good that the work could extend well past the estimate.

In our daily lives we have a simple way of handling variability. For example, if we wished to guess the height of boys in a sixth-grade class, we might say the height is 58 inches, plus or minus 9 inches. In essence we are saying that the heights of almost all the boys will probably fall between 49 and 67 inches. If the class were large, a graph of their heights might look similar to the one found in Figure 8-1. Statisticians call this a normal distribution or a bell curve. Instead of measuring the uncertainty of the estimate with plus or minus a certain percent, they use a measure called the *standard deviation* to measure dispersion or variation. If the variation is known, the percentage of cases above or below any point in the normal distribution can be computed by using standardized tables. The tables, developed by mathematicians, assume that for practical purposes the area under the bell curve equals the whole population—or 1.00. They have proven that if the curve is cut in half, plus or minus one standard deviation from the middle (average) represents about 68 percent of all the cases in the population; plus or minus two standard deviations is approximately 95 percent; and plus or minus three standard deviations is greater than 99 percent. See Figure 8-2. The importance of this information can be shown in the distribution of heights in the sixth-grade class. Assume that the standard deviation is known to be 3 inches. What percentage of the boys would you expect to be less than 58 inches? The answer is 50 percent. What percentage would you expect to be less than 55 inches? Answer, 17 percent. What percentage would you expect to fall below 61 inches? Answer, 84 percent. This same approach will be used to compute the probability of completing a project successfully by a scheduled deadline.

EXPECTED ACTIVITY TIMES

PERT uses three time estimates to compute the average or expected time (t_e). Recall that in the CPM method the expected activity time is a single-point estimate that assumes certainty. PERT time estimates are called *optimistic*, *most likely*, and *pessimistic* times. In practice the most likely time is usually estimated first because it provides a base for deriving the optimistic and pessimistic times. It is important that estimators and management have a clear understanding of the meaning of these times and that they are not confused with early start and late finish times.

1. Most likely time (m): the activity time which is likely to occur most often if the activity were repeated again and again under identical conditions.

2. Optimistic time (a): the minimum time to complete an activity under the most ideal conditions so that there is only one chance in 100 of completing the activity in less than the optimistic time.

3. Pessimistic time (b): the maximum time required to complete an activity if unusual delays arise; there should be only one chance in 100 of the activity taking more than the pessimistic time.

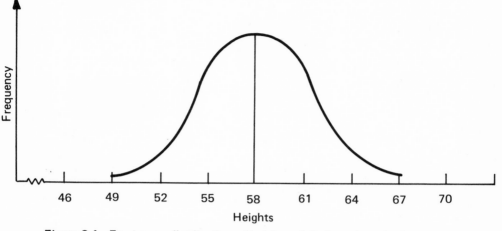

Figure 8-1 Frequency distribution of heights of sixth-grade male students

All of these times should *not* include acts of God; that is, earthquakes, floods, fires, strikes, or other unpredictable catastrophes should not be considered when making a time estimate because there is less than one chance in 100 of any one of them occurring. However, delivery delays, "normal" weather conditions, employee training, and other normal operating conditions that are significant, predictable factors should be included in the time estimate. The optimistic (*a*) and pessimistic (*b*) times should not be confused with the early start (*ES*) and late finish (*LF*) times. Optimistic and pessimistic times have one chance in 100 of occurring; early start occurs if all preceding activities start on their *ES* times, and late finish occurs if all preceding activities are completed on their *LF* times.

Once the three time estimates have been collected, they are averaged by this equation:

(1) $t_e = \dfrac{a+4m+b}{6}$ where t_e = expected (weighted average) activity time

a = optimistic time

m = most likely time

b = pessimistic time

This equation weights the most likely value four times and the optimistic and pessimistic values less because of their small chance of occurring. An

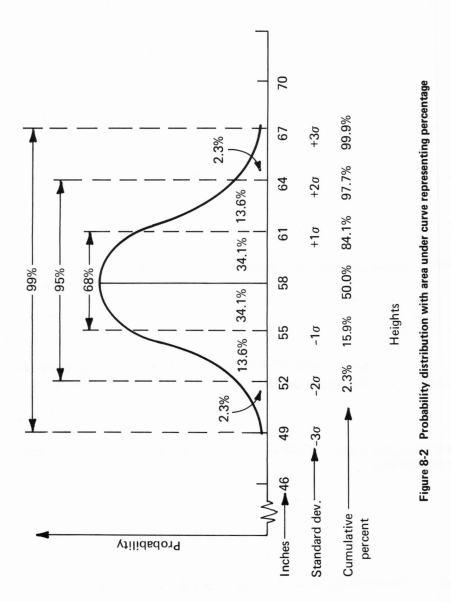

Figure 8-2   Probability distribution with area under curve representing percentage

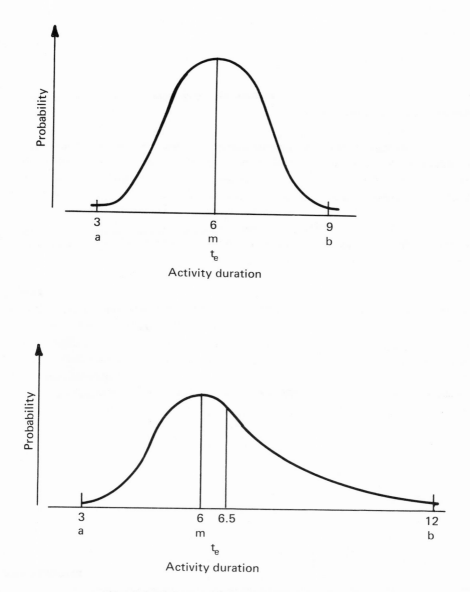

Figure 8-3 Shape of activity distributions

intuitive question that comes to mind when this equation is introduced is, Why don't we add the three times and divide by three? Basically, the answer lies in the fact that work and waiting often cannot be described by a bell curve that is perfectly symmetrical.

Consider the distributions shown in Figure 8-3. The distribution above is a bell curve and is symmetrical. The most likely value is also the average value—[3+4(6)+9]/6=6. The average is defined as the time value in the distribution for which there is a 50-50 chance of getting the task done early or late. The distribution below is more typical of work and waiting. Work has two characteristics which may cause the distribution to have this shape. First, time required for work can be compressed only so far; beyond that point compression is impossible. For example, good driving conditions can shorten driving from one town to another, but the time can be reduced only so far. Second, once work gets behind it tends to drag out, for example, a piece of equipment breaks down and parts are not available. This characteristic causes the distribution to "skew" to the right. The developers of PERT were aware of this phenomenon and the fact that under special conditions the task might even be skewed to the left. To accommodate the fact that if an activity were repeated over and over the frequency of activity times might not be symmetrical, equation (1) is used to compute the weighted average (the expected activity time which has a 50-50 chance of occurring before or after the time). The weighted average time for the activity below is [3+4(6)+12]/6=6.5 weeks. Note that the most likely time (m) is not the same as the expected activity time (t_e). This approximation equation has its genesis in the *beta* distribution, which is beyond the scope of this book; practitioners have found the equation realistic and easy to use, and have found no reason to use another distribution or method. With this background, let us turn to the computational method which is best illustrated with an example.

PERT COMPUTATIONAL PROCEDURE

EXPECTED ACTIVITY TIMES

Assume that the identification of activities, determination of sequence and relationships, and numbering of activities have been completed. The next step is to collect the optimistic, most likely, and pessimistic times from the person most knowledgeable about each task and then compute the expected activity time. This should be done for each activity. Table 8-1 presents the three activity times for a hypothetical problem. The expected activity times are computed using equation (1). These time estimates can now be placed on the network diagram.

TABLE 8-1.   COMPUTED EXPECTED ACTIVITY TIMES.
(weeks)

Activity	Optimistic time (*a*)	Most likely time (*m*)	Pessimistic time (*b*)	t_e $\dfrac{a+4m+b}{6}$		Expected activity time
1-2	7	7	7	$\dfrac{7+4(7)+7}{6}$	=	7.0
1-3	20	20	20	$\dfrac{20+4(20)+20}{6}$	=	20.0
1-4	10	12	20	$\dfrac{10+4(12)+20}{6}$	=	13.0
1-5	36	39	48	$\dfrac{36+4(39)+48}{6}$	=	40.0
2-4	20	29	44	$\dfrac{20+4(29)+44}{6}$	=	30.0
3-5	6	12	18	$\dfrac{6+4(12)+18}{6}$	=	12.0
4-5	11	20	29	$\dfrac{11+4(20)+29}{6}$	=	20.0

Figure 8-4 shows the sample network with the time estimates inserted. The numbers above the activity arrows are the optimistic, most likely, and pessimistic values, respectively. The number below the arrows is the computed expected activity time. The early and late start times for each event have been computed using the procedures of chapter 3. The critical path is 1, 2, 4, 5 and the expected time for the project is 57 weeks. Now we can move to the next step.

PROBABILITY OF COMPLETING AN EVENT SUCCESSFULLY

PERT assumes that each activity and each path has a probability distribution. It assumes that the activity probability distribution can take a variety of shapes, while the probability distribution for a path will be a normal or symmetrical distribution. The project duration is the sum of the average activity times along the longest path; there is an equal chance of the project being completed earlier or later than the critical path time. Variability in project completion time depends on the degree of variability in the durations of the individual activities on the critical path. Variability in project and activity times is measured by the standard deviation.

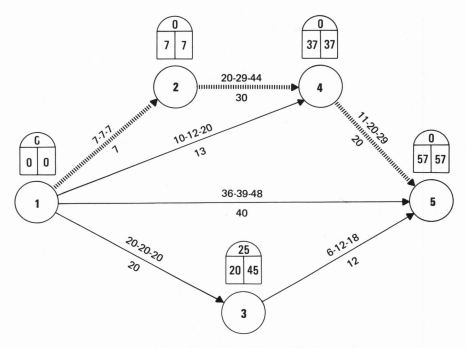

Figure 8-4   Example problem with time estimates

The standard deviation for an *activity* is computed with the expression below:

$$(2) \quad \sigma_{t_e} = \left(\frac{b-a}{6}\right)$$

where σ_{t_e} = standard deviation for *activity*
b = pessimistic time
a = optimistic time

Hence, the standard deviation of activity 4-5 in Figure 8-4 is $(29-11)/6 = 3.0$. Note that the most likely time is not considered.

The expected length of the critical path (T_E) is computed by summing all the expected (average) activity times (t_e). The standard deviation for the critical path is not simply the sum of the activity standard deviations, however. The actual early and late finish times of several activities connected in a series would tend to cancel each other; consequently, the variability for the project duration cannot be the sum of the activity standard deviations; this would be too large. Mathematicians using PERT knew of this problem and developed the equation below which accounts for the cancellation of early and late finish dates of activities connected in a series. The standard deviation for the *project* is as follows:

(3) $\sigma T_E = \sqrt{\Sigma \sigma t_e^2}$

σT_E = standard deviation for *project* or ending event

$\sqrt{}$ = square root

Σ = sum

$\sigma_{t_e}^2$ = *activity* standard deviation squared—also called variance; includes only activities on path being considered

When the expected project completion time and the standard deviation of the activities on the critical path are found, the probability of completing the project by a scheduled deadline is easily computed. The probability can be determined by finding the Z factor in the expression below and then finding the probability in a standardized table:

(4) $Z = \dfrac{T_S - T_E}{\sqrt{\Sigma \sigma t_e^2}}$ where

T_S = scheduled event time

T_E = expected event time

$\sqrt{\Sigma \sigma t_e^2}$ = square root of sum of activity variances on the path being considered or standard deviation of path

Let us illustrate with the example in Figure 8-4 by finding the probability of meeting a scheduled date of 59 weeks for the project. The expected project time is 57 weeks, which has a 50-percent change of being met; hence, we know the chance of 59 weeks is more than 50 percent—but how much more? The question is posed graphically in Figure 8-5.

The probability is equal to the shaded area under the curve to the left of 59 weeks. How much of the bell curve does the shaded (probability) area cover? By finding the Z value from equation (4) we can convert this value to the probability from a standardized table. The first step is to find activity standard deviations and variances. Table 8-2 shows the computed activity standard deviations and variances for each activity. To compute the Z value, simply plug in the values needed for equation (4). The computations are given below:

$$Z = \frac{T_S - T_E}{\sqrt{\Sigma \sigma t_e^2}} = \frac{59 - 57}{\sqrt{0 + 16 + 9}} = \frac{+2}{\sqrt{25}} = +\frac{2}{5} = +.40$$

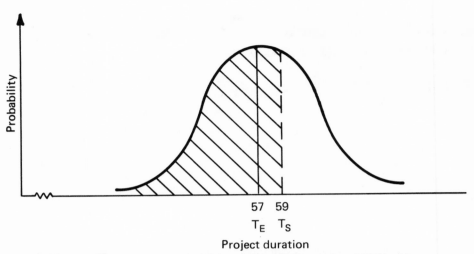

57   59
T_E T_S
Project duration

Figure 8-5 Probability of completing project in 59 weeks

TABLE 8-2. ACTIVITY STANDARD DEVIATIONS AND VARIANCES.

Activity	Time estimates a	m	b	t_e	Activity standard deviation $\left(\dfrac{b-a}{6}\right)$	Variance (standard deviation squared)* $\left(\dfrac{b-a}{6}\right)^2$
1-2	7	7	7	7	$\left(\dfrac{7-7}{6}\right) = 0$	$\left(0\right)^2 = 0$
1-3	20	20	20	20	$\left(\dfrac{20-20}{6}\right) = 0$	$\left(0\right)^2 = 0$
1-4	10	12	20	13	$\left(\dfrac{20-10}{6}\right) = \dfrac{5}{3}$	$\left(\dfrac{5}{3}\right)^2 = \dfrac{25}{9} = 2.78$
1-5	36	39	48	40	$\left(\dfrac{36-48}{6}\right) = 2.0$	$\left(2.0\right)^2 = 4.00$
2-4	20	29	44	30	$\left(\dfrac{44-20}{6}\right) = 4.0$	$\left(4.0\right)^2 = 16.00$
3-5	6	12	18	12	$\left(\dfrac{18-6}{6}\right) = 2.0$	$\left(2.0\right)^2 = 4.00$
4-5	11	20	29	20	$\left(\dfrac{29-11}{6}\right) = 3.0$	$\left(3.0\right)^2 = 9.00$

* See Appendix for tables of the squares of numbers.

(The square roots of numbers are found in the Appendix.) Observe that the sum of the variances includes only those activities on the critical path. Given a Z value of +.40 we can turn to the standardized probability tables found in Table 8-3. A Z value of +.40 corresponds to a probability of .655 or 65 percent. This means that given the variability of individual activity times along the critical path in the problem, the chances of completing this project in 59 weeks are .65 or 65 chances out of 100.

Let us try two more problems for practice. What is the probability of finishing this project in 54 weeks? Figure 8-6 shows the problem graphically. The Z value is computed below:

$$Z = \frac{54-57}{\sqrt{0+16+9}} = \frac{-3}{\sqrt{25}} = \frac{-3}{5} = -.60$$

From Table 8-3 the chance of completing the project successfully by 54 weeks is 27 percent. Another kind of question can be asked: What is the probability of completing path 1,3,5 in 30 weeks? The Z value is computed as follows:

$$Z = \frac{30-32}{\sqrt{0+4}} = \frac{-2}{\sqrt{4}} = \frac{-2}{+2} = -1.0$$

From Table 8-3 the probability is .16 or 16 percent. Thus we can find the probability of any event by using the square root of the sum of the standard deviations of the activities on the longest path leading to the ending event. Note that when T_S is less than T_E, the corresponding probability will be less than .50; when T_S is greater than T_E, the probability will be greater than .50.

HANDLING NEAR-CRITICAL PATHS

The procedures given above work well in most projects. When near-critical paths exist, some caution should be used. If we deal only with the critical path, we could compute probabilities that are overly optimistic. How can this happen? An example will illustrate. Assume a project where the duration of the critical path is 36 weeks and the standard deviation for the path is three weeks. Another near-critical path exists with an expected duration of 34 weeks and a standard deviation of six weeks for its path. Figure 8-7 illustrates this situation graphically. If the contract calls for completion of the project in 37 weeks, what is the probability of complet-

TABLE 8-3.   PROBABILITY OF MEETING SCHEDULED DATE.

T_S less than T_E		T_S greater than T_E	
Z	Probability	Z	Probability
-3.0	.001	+0.0	.500
-2.9	.002	+0.1	.540
-2.8	.003	+0.2	.579
-2.7	.004	+0.3	.618
-2.6	.005	+0.4	.655
-2.5	.006	+0.5	.692
-2.4	.008	+0.6	.726
-2.3	.011	+0.7	.758
-2.2	.014	+0.8	.788
-2.1	.018	+0.9	.816
-2.0	.023	+1.0	.841
-1.9	.029	+1.1	.864
-1.8	.036	+1.2	.885
-1.7	.045	+1.3	.903
-1.6	.055	+1.4	.919
-1.5	.067	+1.5	.933
-1.4	.081	+1.6	.945
-1.3	.097	+1.7	.955
-1.2	.115	+1.8	.964
-1.1	.136	+1.9	.971
-1.0	.159	+2.0	.977
-0.9	.184	+2.1	.982
-0.8	.212	+2.2	.986
-0.7	.242	+2.3	.989
-0.6	.274	+2.4	.992
-0.5	.309	+2.5	.994
-0.4	.345	+2.6	.995
-0.3	.382	+2.7	.997
-0.2	.421	+2.8	.997
-0.1	.460	+2.9	.998

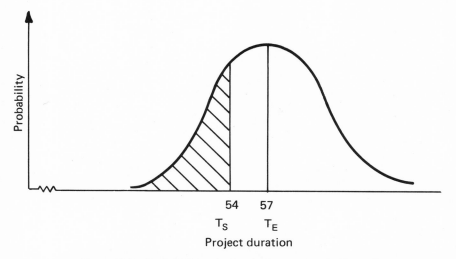

Figure 8-6 Probability of completing project in 54 weeks

ing it in this time? Normally, we would ignore all noncritical paths and compute the Z factor as follows:

$$Z = \frac{T_S - T_E}{\sqrt{\Sigma \, \sigma_{t_e}^{\,2}}} = \frac{37 - 36}{3} = \frac{+1}{+3} = +.33$$

From Table 8-3 the probability is .64 or 64 percent of completing the project in 37 weeks. This approach assumes that the other paths will not affect the completion date. But it is possible for the near-critical path to be late—say, three weeks and take 37 weeks. The Z factor of the near-critical path being completed in 37 weeks is shown below:

$$Z = \frac{37 - 34}{6} = \frac{+3}{+6} = +.50$$

From Table 8-3 the probability is .69 of meeting the 37-week schedule. Clearly, if the schedule is to be 37 weeks, it depends on the chances of *both* paths being completed by this deadline. The probability of both paths being completed in 37 weeks depends on their joint probability, found by multiplying the probabilities of meeting each date times the other. In this case the joint probability is .64x.69=.44—a probability which is not as optimistic as the probability of .64 found using only the critical path.

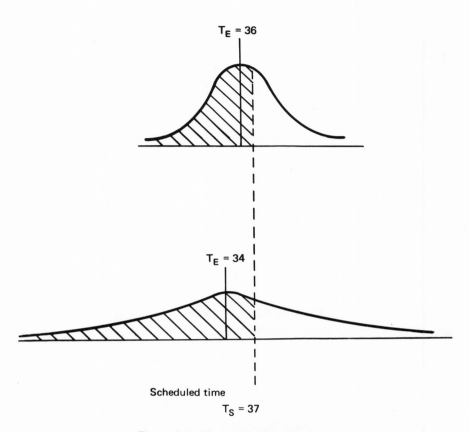

Figure 8-7   Near-critical path projects

The problem of near-critical paths can be significant when the variance along these paths is large relative to the critical path. The standard critical path approach works well where the critical path is dominant or where parallel paths have few interconnections. However, when near-critical paths have large variance relative to those found on the critical path, there is a good chance of overstating the probability of meeting a deadline. Furthermore, to the manager near-critical paths mean the chances are good for shifting critical paths and for unforeseen problems occurring.

A better alternative to the joint probability method, and one which makes fewer assumptions, is to simulate the network. Simulation uses the same information needed for PERT, but it utilizes the information better and provides more reliable output. PERT simulation is the topic of the next chapter.

USEFULNESS OF PERT INFORMATION

The ability of management to associate a probability with a completion date for any event in the network provides them with a useful, powerful tool. Probabilities of completion dates direct management's attention to potential bottlenecks. The probabilities are useful in contract negotiation in setting completion dates, assessing incentive and penalty clauses, and assigning risk levels. Probabilities of completion allow management to adjust resources levels in the planning stages to increase the probability of meeting a deadline. PERT information appears to be most valuable in those projects which have a high degree of uncertainty associated with their activities and a high penalty for being wrong.

QUESTIONS

8-1. What are the basic differences between PERT and CPM?

8-2. Why does the PERT system use a *beta* distribution?

8-3. Why doesn't PERT deal with the dynamics of the project?

EXERCISES

8-1. Given the information in the table below, answer the following:

   (a) Compute the expected time for each activity (t_e).
   (b) Identify the critical path.
   (c) Compute the variance for each activity (σ^2).
   (d) Compute the expected project duration (T_E).
   (e) Compute the probability of completing the project within 74 days.

ACTIVITY	a	m	b
1-2	6	12	24
1-3	2	5	8
2-4	20	35	50
3-4	1	1	1
3-5	17	29	47
4-6	13	16	19
5-6	16	19	28
6-7	4	7	10

8-2. Given the network information below for the Corporate Consolidation, compute the following:

(a) Expected time for each activity
(b) Variance for each activity
(c) Project duration
(d) Probability of completing the project by day 112; within 116 days
(e) Probability of completing "Negotiate with Unions" by day 90.

ACTIVITY	DESCRIPTION	a	m	b
1-2	Codify accounts	16	19	28
1-5	File articles of unification	30	30	30
1-6	Unify price & credit policy	60	72	90
1-7	Unify personnel policies	18	27	30
2-3	Unify data processing	17	29	47
2-4	Train accounting staff	4	7	10
3-4	Pilot run data processing	12	15	18
4-8	Calculate P&L and balance sheet	6	12	24
5-10	Transfer real property	18	27	30
6-11	Train salesforce	20	35	50
7-9	Negotiate with unions	40	55	100
8-10	Determine capital needs	11	20	29
9-11	Explain new personnel policies	14	23	26
10-11	Secure line of credit	13	16	19

8-3. The expected activity times and the activity variances are given for each activity in this new product development project. What is the probability of completing the project within 25 weeks?

ACTIVITY	DESCRIPTION	DURATION (t_e)	VARIANCE (σ^2)
1-2	Design package	5	2
1-3	Design product	16	11
2-4	Build package	10	5
3-4	Build product	4	2
4-5	Test market	8	3

8-4. Assume the information below from a PERT network is given. Compute the probability of completing the project in 29 weeks.

ACTIVITY	t_e	VARIANCE (σ^2)
1-2	11	9
1-3	10	20
1-4	7	12
2-5	4	1
3-5	16	10
4-5	5	16
5-6	5	6
5-7	2	4
6-7	0	0

8-5. Information from a PERT network is given below. Compute the probability of completing the project within 99 days. Within 105 days.

ACTIVITY	a	m	b
1-2	17	29	47
1-3	18	27	30
1-4	7	9	10
2-5	3	5	6
3-5	12	15	18
3-6	2	3	5
3-7	4	7	10
4-6	2	4	7
5-7	40	55	100
6-7	2	4	4

9
PERT Simulation

THIS CHAPTER* describes the PERT Simulation (PS) technique which allows the manager to cope with the uncertainty and instability inherent in the time estimates that are used for planning the project. By simulating the PERT network, the PS model reveals the likelihood of shifting critical paths while the project is in the early planning stages. First we shall examine the PERT problem and the need for the added dimension of network dynamics. This is followed by a nontechnical description of the method used to transform the standard PERT model to PS. Third, some of the key points of network analysis with PS are noted; two examples of applications are described and a list of advantages is presented. Finally, a so-called rough simulation approach is discussed.

THE PERT PROBLEM

The standard PERT approach as presented in the previous chapter does not cope adequately with the uncertainty and instability associated with estimates of activity times and the resultant determination of project completion time. For example, in the standard PERT analysis an activity time es-

---

* Much of the material in this chapter (including figures 9-1 through 9-6 and tables 9-1 and 9-2) was developed previously for an article in the *Journal for Systems Management*, "PERT Simulation: A Dynamic Approach to the PERT Technique," by Clifford Gray and Robert Reiman (March 1969), pp. 18–23. Used by permission.

timate may be described by optimistic (*a*), most likely (*m*), and pessimistic (*b*) values of 10, 15, and 26. The mean of the activity duration time is calculated by the PERT method

$$t_e = \frac{a+4m+b}{6}$$

Thus the expected time is 16. The mean value for each activity in the network is calculated by this formula, and the duration time for the total project is ascertained by the addition of the activity times along the longest path through the network. Even though this method uses a *beta* distribution and an expected value, it is a deterministic method because the activity time is treated as a single static value.

Unfortunately, a great deal of uncertainty surrounds activity duration time estimates in an actual project portrayed by a PERT network. In the example above (10, 15, 26), the activity duration time may be expected to occur at some value between 10 and 26 (and in rare cases may actually go beyond these extremes). As the activity time varies within this range, it may have an effect on the entire network of interrelated activities, even to the extent of completely altering the critical path configuration. Each activity in the network may have just such a potential effect.

For example, what happens if the activity is not completed until the twenty-fifth day? Does the critical path stay the same or does it change? Standard PERT techniques shed little light on this important question. In a large, complex network with several paths having project duration times that are nearly the same length, the probability of the critical path shifting to other paths is high. In a real project situation that has several closely timed critical paths, the actual critical path may swing back and forth between the several paths many times during the actual course of the project work. It would be especially useful to be aware of the possible critical paths that might occur in the planning and bidding stages of the project.

INTRODUCTION TO PS

PS accounts for the actual duration time associated with each activity as being some value lying within optimistic-to-pessimistic time estimates but with some form of probability distribution over the range, rather than being simply a specified deterministic time. PS incorporates this variance or element of uncertainty dynamically into the analysis. By simulating this variance the PS model reveals the likelihood of shifting critical paths in advance by determining the relative probabilities of each network activity and of each alternative path becoming critical.

Thus, planning can be refined in advance to reduce the incidence of bottlenecks not detected by the standard PERT analysis. PS can greatly expand the application of management by exception in project management and can reduce brush fire situations to a minimum.

The accuracy of PS is greater than that of PERT. The standard PERT assumes a *beta* distribution, but the true distribution is unknown. PS allows a manager to select the distribution judged to fit the situation best, for example, *beta*, normal, triangular, rectangular, or even specially programmed empirical distributions for special jobs. The manager can select any mix of distributions.

Different job activity estimates undoubtedly have differently shaped probability distributions. The estimator who provides the time estimates for a particular activity has an intuitive or subjective feeling, or even an empirical reference from personal experience, with which to judge the shape of the probability distribution for the activity. Because a selection from alternative distribution forms is provided, the manager has more complete and reliable data available to utilize in the model.

Although the PERT network configuration depicts clearly and concisely the interrelationships of all the project activities and events, the PERT analysis, being a deterministic solution using a static model, does not take into account the interaction inherent in these interrelated activities. PS converts the PERT network into a dynamic model of the project activities and thereby reflects the interaction within the network as well as the interrelationships; it models the real project situation accurately.

PS AND THE MONTE CARLO METHOD

The conversion of the static PERT model into a dynamic one is done by applying the Monte Carlo (simulated sampling) method. This method makes it possible to manipulate the PERT model of the project and predict how the real system might behave. Monte Carlo uses random numbers to generate simulated activity times for each activity in the network.

For each simulation trial, the generated activity time for each activity will be early, on schedule, or late relative to the expected duration time (t_e) for the activity. The particular time selected will be dependent on the random number and the selected probability distribution. With these factors given for each activity, the model should come up with about the same relative frequency of activity duration times as would occur in the real world. However, the duration times in the model would be "randomized."

By simulating the network several hundred times, each time randomly selecting an activity time from within its estimated range for each activity, one can find the probability of an activity being on any critical path that might occur and the probability of any particular critical path occurring. These probability or criticality indices are very useful as an indication of the degree of management attention an activity should receive, and in allocation of resources to ensure completion of an activity on schedule.

PS AND THE COMPUTER

The PS system requires a computer to execute the simulation, and more time is required to run PS than to run standard PERT. This limitation is less serious as additional and faster computer facilities and hardware become available through computer service centers and through remote access to time-sharing groups. With only a few minor exceptions the information needed for PS is identical to that needed for standard PERT calculations. Most library PS computer programs provide the standard PERT output if desired—critical path, slack times, and bar charts—plus other valuable information that comes from a Monte Carlo simulation of the PERT network several hundred times.

AN EXAMPLE OF MONTE CARLO APPLIED

A simple example will illustrate how the Monte Carlo simulation method operates and will demonstrate what the computer program does to simulate a network. Figure 9-1 is a simple PERT network. The optimistic, most likely, and pessimistic times are given for each activity. For simplicity of demonstration, assume that the probability distribution describing the possible time durations for the completion of an activity is a normal distribution and the range is finite.* Figure 9-2 is a graphic representation of the normal distribution form for the two specified ranges of activity time estimates. With the range of the activity time estimates specified, and assuming the area under the curve to be equal to one, the probability of completing a job by a particular day can be determined by using standard statistical tables for the normal distribution. For example, in Part A the probability of completing the activity in 10 days or less is $p=.02$; in 11 days or less, $p=.16$; in 14 days or less, $p=98$; in 15 days or less, $p=1.00$; the same procedure applies to Part (b).

Figure 9-3 is a cumulative presentation of the distributions in Figure 9-2. In both distributions 50 percent of the curve is above and 50 percent is below the mean value (12 or 23). With the cumulative probability distributions established for each activity as in Figure 9-3, the network can be re-

*Standard PERT assumes a *beta* distribution. In the strictest sense, normal distributions are not finite.

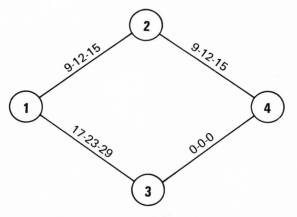

Figure 9-1 Simple PERT network

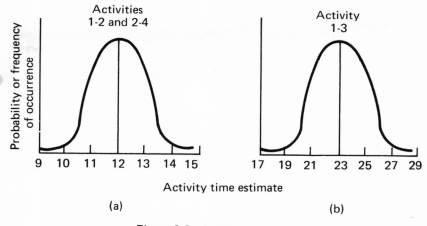

Figure 9-2 Activity distributions

produced manually. For PS the hand simulation procedure can be broken into five steps:

1. Generate a random number for each activity. (This can be done by randomly drawing chips numbered between 00 and 99—representing probabilities—from a box, or by using a table or random digits.)

2. Sample the specific cumulative distribution to determine a simulated activity duration time for each activity.

3. Record the simulated duration time for each activity.

4. Determine the critical path when duration times for all activities in the network have been simulated.

5. Record critical activities and critical paths.

Assume the first random number drawn for activity 1-2 is 16 (see Figure 9-3). Find the cumulative probability on the vertical scale that corresponds to the random number; this number is $p = .16$. Follow across the graph horizontally until intersecting the curve; then move down to the horizontal scale and read the activity duration time—the duration time for activity 1-2 is 11.0 weeks. Record the duration time and follow the same procedure for the other activities in the network. Table 9-1 gives the results of three simulations. The path taking the longest time for completion is labeled critical.

From this information a criticality index for each possible critical path and each activity is calculated. Figure 9-1 shows that the network contains only two possible critical paths—1, 2, 4 and 1, 3, 4. Table 9-1 indicates that in three simulations, path 1, 3, 4 was critical once, and 1, 2, 4 twice. Thus, after three simulations, the criticality index or probability of path 1, 2, 4 being critical is $p = .67$ or 67 percent, while for path 1, 3, 4 it is $p = .33$ or 33 percent.

The same process is used to calculate the criticality index for each activity, or the probability that a given activity will be on a critical path. The

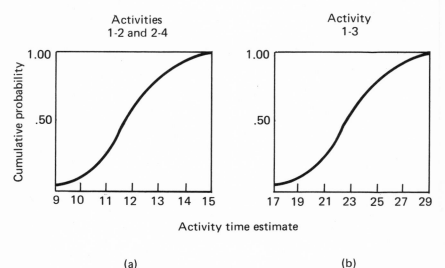

(a)   (b)

Figure 9-3   Cumulative activity distributions

criticality index for each activity and path is listed in Table 9-2 for the example with three simulations. Since three simulations would not generally yield reliable information, the table also contains the same information from a computer run when the network was simulated 2,500 times.

Of course, if the network were larger and more complex, the indices for the paths probably would be different from those found for most activities, since the number of possible critical paths could increase tremendously.

NETWORK ANALYSIS

Figure 9-4 shows the original example network with the probability of the activities becoming critical listed also. Using the PERT procedure, the critical path is clearly 1, 2, 4. However, when the variance element of the activity is incorporated by PS and a criticality index is determined for each activity, management's feeling about the critical path is probably tempered.

TABLE 9-1. NETWORK SIMULATION.

Activity	SIMULATION 1			SIMULATION 2			SIMULATION 3		
	Random Number	Activity Duration	Critical Activity	Random Number	Activity Duration	Critical Activity	Random Number	Activity Duration	Critical Activity
1-2	16	11.0		65	12.4	*	6	10.5	*
1-3	84	25.0	*	5	19.8		24	21.6	
2-4	69	12.5		59	12.2	*	55	12.1	*
3-4	—	0.0	*	—	0.0		—	0.0	

* Critical Activity.

TABLE 9-2. CRITICALITY INDICES.

Activity	Critical Index 3 Simulations (by hand)	Critical Index 2,500 Simulations (by computer)
1-2	.67	.627
1-3	.33	.373
2-4	.67	.627
3-4	.33	.373
path		
1-2-4	.67	.627
1-3-4	.33	.373

It is likely that management would now direct more attention to activity 1-3, since the likelihood of its being on the critical path is $p=.373$ (a 37 percent chance). In a large, complex project with management's attention directed primarily to the critical path, and with firm resources—money, labor, and materials—devoted to activities on the critical path, some very costly mistakes can occur. The criticality index concept is exceedingly useful in directing attention to areas where bottlenecks might occur *before* the project begins and in allocating scarce resources.

The criticality concept alerts management to potential bottlenecks that are not apparent when using PERT and its resulting critical path. An activity with a relatively high criticality index possibly may not appear on the PERT critical path. Activity 1-2 in Figure 9-5 with a probabilty of $p=.360$ is more critical than activity 3-7 (which is on the critical path).[1] Such weaknesses in the PERT-calculated critical path concept make the case for the criticality concept even stronger.

PS identifies those activities that cannot become critical or are almost never critical. This information is not revealed in PERT, although it can be determined. Such information is valuable to management, since attention can then be directed safely to activities which need the most consideration.

One word of caution is necessary for those who choose the criticality index concept to analyze PERT networks. A relatively low activity criticality index, such as $p=.20$, does not necessarily mean it is unimportant. If we assume the sample network in Figure 9-6, the point is obvious. It should be clear that each activity has one chance in five of being critical; hence $p=.20$. Since each activity is equally important, all should probably receive equal attention. In large, complex networks the greater the number of parallel paths with similar project duration times, the smaller will be the probability of activities occurring on these related paths. Thus the criticality indices should be viewed as relative to all the other probabilities in the network in order to evaluate their importance as critical elements in the project.

The Corporate Consolidation of problem 8-2 is shown in Figure 9-7. The critical path is 1, 2, 3, 4, 8, 10, 11; the duration by standard PERT is 114 days. Figure 9-8 shows the output for the PS computer program. Note that

---

1. Since there is no strong empirical base for using the *beta* distribution, the author used the triangular distribution to simulate the networks discussed. The simulation results for the beta and triangular distributions are similar. For more detail on the mathematical development, see Kenneth R. MacCrimmon and Charles A. Ryavec, "An Analytical Study of the PERT Assumptions," in *Operations Research* January-February 1964, Vol. 12, No. 1, pp. 16-37; Richard M. Van Slyke, "Monte Carlo Methods and the PERT Problem," *Operations Research*, September-October 1963, Vol. II, No. 5, pp. 839-860; R. Lowell Wine, *Statistics for Scientists and Engineers* (Englewood Cliffs, N.J.: Prentice-Hall, 1964), pp. 71-73; Thomas H. Naylor, Joseph L. Balintey, Donald S. Burdick and Kong Cha, *Computer Simulation Techniques* (New York: John Wiley, 1967), pp. 77-80.

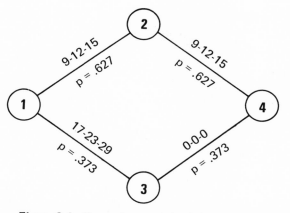

Figure 9-4   Example network with criticality indices

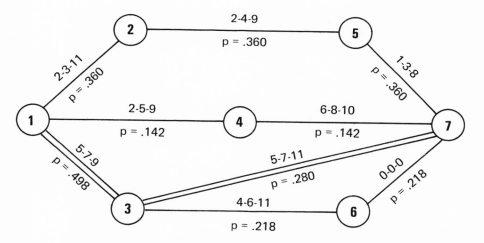

Figure 9-5   Computer-simulated network with criticality indices

three critical paths occurred when the network was simulated and that the project duration times for all three critical paths were greater than the expected time for the PERT critical path—114 days. The difference is caused by the large positive bias in the activities. This network would be considered "sensitive," since the probability of the other two paths occurring is high, relative to the critical path. In actual practice, parallel paths with similar project duration times are not the exception; this situation occurs quite frequently.

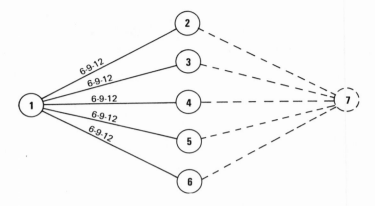

Figure 9-6   Low criticality indices

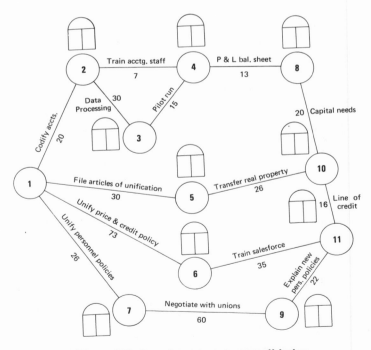

Figure 9-7   Sample corporate consolidation

SAMPLE CORPORATE CONSOLIDATION

Analysis of Critical Paths From PERT Simulation
Number of Critical Paths Resulting=3

Critical Path ID No.	No. of Activities	No. Times Critical	Probability	Average Total Time
1	6	106	.530	118.7
2	2	40	.200	122.0
3	3	54	.270	125.8

Critical Path ID No. 1

Activities: 1-2, 2-3, 3-4, 4-8, 8-10, 10-11

Critical Path ID No. 2

Activities: 1-6, 6-11

Critical Path ID No. 3

Activities: 1-7, 7-9, 9-11

Figure 9-8   Computer output

APPLICATIONS OF PS

Two examples of application provide insight into the latent power of PS
in developing a wealth of information to guide management in the planning
stages of a project. While neither of these projects is especially complex or
lengthy, each illustrates one extreme in project sensitivity as revealed by
the PS model.

HIGHWAY DESIGN PROJECT

An engineering design firm used standard PERT for planning a large highway
design project. In addition to the most likely time, the estimators provided

the minimum possible completion time and the maximum time for completion, both based on reasonably foreseeable circumstances that would give cause for these extremes. The standard PERT network established sequences and related the 94 activities of the project. The critical path or longest path for the network was found by the standard technique.

These same highway design project data were run through the PS model. Criticality or probability of occurrence for both the activities the critical paths was calculated. Results of the simulation of this project network were particularly revealing in that a total of 88 unique, critical paths resulted. Thus an apparently insensitive network was revealed to be highly sensitive. The particular path having the highest criticality index was, indeed, the path calculated by the standard PERT technique. But its probability of being the critical path was only 11.5 percent.

The above results of the PS analysis for this design project are meaningful mainly in revealing the relative sensitivity of a given project network schedule. They also illustrate the inadequacy of the static PERT and CPM methods in detecting sensitivity and accounting for variances and uncertainty. But these results, by themselves, do not provide sufficient information to guide management in implementing specific planning action to anticipate critical problem areas in the project network. Further information is generated by the PS model to identify specific critical points for management attention. This is accomplished by the concept of a criticality or probability index for each activity in the network.

Table 9-3 lists the PS program output for the criticality index of each activity in the network. It can be seen that the criticality indices vary from zero to .999 (or 1.00). Of the 94 scheduled activities (the others were dummy activities), 51 were not on any critical path while 6 were always critical. With this information, management formulated and implemented specific action plans, and attention was directed and pinpointed with greater accuracy, reliability, and confidence. The planning spectrum became a continuum with the predetermined emphasis of direction and intensity rather than a blanket effort calculated to cover expected but unidentified deviation from a given critical path with only a questionable likelihood of being realized.

PRODUCT AND PROCESS DEVELOPMENT PROJECT

The second example of PS application is the complete development of a company structure—beginning with the decision "to produce a balanced line of high-quality, dehydrated food ingredients for manufacturers of consumer food products." The project involved such activities as designing the physical plant and production processes, building a management organiza-

TABLE 9-3.   CRITICALITY INDICES FOR PROJECT ACTIVITIES.

Activity	Criticality Index	Activity	Criticality Index	Activity	Criticality Index
1- 2	.238	26-27	.000	53-54	.162
1- 3	.544	26-28	.270	53-55	.044
1- 4	.222	27-30	.730	54-56	.162
2- 4	.238	28-29	.270	55-58	.044
3- 4	.544	29-30	.270	56-57	.076
4- 5	.036	30-31	.000	56-59	.000
4- 6	.694	30-34	1.000	56-60	.000
4- 9	.268	30-40	.000	56-61	.000
4-10	.000	31-32	.000	56-62	.880
4-13	.000	31-37	.000	57-69	.078
4-14	.000	32-38	.000	58-71	.044
4-15	.002	33-36	.000	59-66	.000
4-16	.000	33-46	.000	60-66	.000
4-17	.000	34-36	1.000	61-66	.000
4-18	.000	34-40	.000	62-63	.880
4-20	.000	35-36	.000	62-65	.000
4-21	.000	35-81	.000	63-66	.880
5- 6	.036	36-37	.002	64-66	.000
6- 7	.730	36-39	.000	65-66	.000
6- 8	.000	36-41	.998	66-67	.000
7- 8	.730	37-38	.002	66-68	.000
8-20	.000	37-68	.000	66-70	.880
8-22	.000	38-45	.002	66-71	.000
8-27	.730	39-41	.000	66-72	.000
9-10	.268	39-42	.000	67-75	.000
9-12	.000	40-41	.000	68-69	.000
10-11	.268	41-43	.998	68-76	.000
11-19	.268	42-71	.000	69-77	.078
12-19	.000	43-44	.000	70-71	.880
12-35	.000	43-45	.000	71-73	.000
14-19	.000	43-47	.998	71-74	.924
15-19	.002	44-67	.000	72-79	.000
16-19	.000	45-57	.002	73-78	.000
17-33	.000	46-53	.000	74-75	.000

TABLE 9-3.   CRITICALITY INDICES FOR PROJECT ACTIVITIES (cont.).

Activity	Criticality Index	Activity	Criticality Index	Activity	Criticality Index
18-44	.000	46-64	.000	74-76	.304
19-23	.000	47-48	.000	74-78	.620
19-24	.000	47-49	.000	75-81	.000
19-25	.000	47-50	.000	76-77	.304
19-26	.270	47-51	.792	76-83	.000
20-21	.000	47-52	.206	77-81	.380
21-32	.000	47-80	.000	78-79	.620
22-36	.000	48-56	.000	79-81	.620
23-26	.000	49-56	.000	80-81	.000
23-30	.000	50-56	.000	81-82	1.000
24-26	.000	51-56	.792	82-83	1.000
24-30	.000	52-53	.206	83-84	1.000
25-26	.000	52-54	.000	84-85	1.000

tion, developing a market, developing the product, setting up pilot production runs, and other activities necessary to start a business based on a new product idea.

The standard PERT network for the project was designed, and times were assigned to the activities. When these time estimates were run through the PS model, the results indicated that the network was insensitive; that is, the actual path calculated by the standard PERT technique occurred in 84.8 percent of the total computer simulations of the network. Only two other unique paths occurred, and they occurred in only 12.2 percent and 3.0 percent, respectively, of the total network simulations. In every case delivery of production equipment turned out to be the bottleneck area. But also in every case the PS model identified the bottlenecks with a relatively high criticality index for those troublesome activities.

In this application of PS, the results regarding the critical path were similar to those found by the standard PERT method. However, the depth of the analysis attained by PS provided valuable insight into the planning schedules and greatly increased the confidence level in implementing the project work. The fact that the project was relatively insensitive to variances in activities not on the main critical path allowed more intensive concentration on the critical activities. The criticality index also revealed those activities that were never critical.

These two examples of highway design and product development illustrate extremes in project sensitivity. They were selected to draw attention to a major point concerning PS, which is that it is equally important for management to know that a network is insensitive to delays or early completion of activities as it is to know that it is sensitive.

ROUGH SIMULATION

Most of the problems encountered in using PERT and PS center around the activity time estimates. The costs of gathering optimistic and pessimistic times have discouraged its use. Some line managers hesitate to give optimistic activity durations because top management tends to want the activity completed by the optimistic time even though there should only be one chance in 100 of doing the job in the optimistic time. Finally, field experience has suggested that the actual activity times average nearly 25 percent higher than the original estimates; furthermore, on occasion time estimates are off as much as 500 percent. The latter makes a good case for PS. One solution to all of these problems has been the use of the "standard job" approach. This method relates each activity in the project to a standard task that is familiar to everyone in the organization. Through a series of questions a relative "distribution" is created for each activity by defining the optimistic and pessimistic times as a percentage of the expected time. Although this approach is not as accurate as the regular approach, it has been used with some success.

CONCLUSIONS

PS is no panacea. Its greatest application has been in the planning stages of project management. But most planning schemes assume that the plan and data are accurate, that the plan will be carried out, and that the future will evolve as planned. Therefore, PS—as most other planning techniques—is primarily dependent on the validity of the information provided. If the inputs to the PS model are updated continually to reflect changes, the model can be very useful for planning, scheduling, and managing large, complex projects.

PS offers many advantages. Some of the main ones are summarized as follows:

1. PS uses essentially the same input data as does standard PERT but also provides a means to incorporate subjective or intuitive factors into the data.

2. It tests the network to identify which paths are sensitive to delays or early completion of activities.

3. It copes with the uncertainty associated with activity duration times and the dynamic interaction between the activities of the closed network.

4. The criticality indices for the activities reveal the likelihood of activities becoming critical *before* the project begins. The indices also serve as an indication of the degree of management attention an activity should receive.

5. Accuracy and flexibility are increased, since any probability distribution or mix of distributions may be used by the estimator.

6. It identifies those activities that will rarely or never occur on any of the possible critical paths.

The criticality concept is more useful for management by exception than the single critical path concept used in network analysis. The criticality indices provide information to assist in the allocation of scarce resources such as labor, money, materials, and equipment. The information derived from PS is valuable to management whether the network is sensitive or insensitive to changes in activity duration times. Since PS fully utilizes the manager's experience and subjective feelings concerning the work of the project, more accurate results are obtained. All of this adds up to improved opportunity for better time and cost performance.

QUESTIONS

9-1. What is the PERT problem?

9-2. What is a criticality index in project management?

9-3. Why is it believed that the criticality index approach is more useful in management by exception than the critical path approach?

9-4. What are the advantages of PERT simulation?

10
Future of Project Management

SINCE the inception of the basic techniques of project management over two decades ago, their use has spread to managers in every country. Surveys show that approximately 70 percent of the manufacturing firms in the United States use PERT/CPM network-based systems. The reasons for their use and success are obvious. The essentials of project management are simple, useful, practical; they fit projects of all sizes, and are applicable to manual or computer solutions. The future holds promise for increasing use of project management techniques by more organizations.

The original techniques have survived these many years with very little modification. However, a great deal of effort and talent have been devoted to extending and refining the original techniques to increase their usefulness. Most of the effort in refinement has been directed toward resource scheduling, cost, organizing for projects, total information systems for projects, graphics, and professionalism for project managers.

RESOURCES

Through 1965 very little emphasis was given to scheduling resources. Prior to this time project managers developed a network plan with very little concern for materials, labor, and equipment. They assumed resources would be available on the dates specified in the plan. Since the likelihood of this occurring would be rare, some applications of project management techniques failed. In the past two decades, practitioners and scholars of project management have been stressing the importance of lining up the resources so they will be available when they are needed and not committed to another project at the same time. Several resource scheduling methods and computer programs have been developed to handle the resource availability problem. The rewards have been great to those astute enough to recognize the resource problem and its importance to project success.

COST

This is another area that is currently receiving more attention. Since most project efforts carry a price tag indicating the expenditure of money, it is natural that project managers would continue to develop new and improved performance measurement schemes. Early in the development of project management techniques the government required (and still does) that contractors for the Department of Defense (DOD), National Aeronautics and Space Administration (NASA), and Department of Energy (DOE) use the Cost/Schedule Control System of the respective agency. This system is being refined and improved constantly. The full potential of cost planning, scheduling, and controlling is only being realized today. Software developers are devoting significant effort and talent to developing cost and quantity packages for managing small projects. This is especially true in the contracting industry where new packages are coming out almost daily. Since the format of these systems is applicable to organizations that are not contractors, it is likely that the current surge will be followed by the development of "generalized packages" that will have wider applicability.

ORGANIZATIONAL ARRANGEMENT

Since most organizations are set up functionally, and since projects are usually implemented by a temporary interdisciplinary team from several functional areas, determining the appropriate organizational arrangement is a question that has yet to be answered. Traditionally, the literature would suggest that the *matrix* organization facilitates the formal authority and responsibility relationships between the functional sections of the organization and the project management team. However, in the past few years the number of articles suggesting alternative organizational arrangements is increasing. Since the new approaches have not been documented, more time is needed. It is probable that this effort will bear fruit in the next decade.

COMPUTER-BASED TOTAL INFORMATION SYSTEMS

The increased availability of computer software and the decreasing costs of hardware, software, and computer operation have all encouraged growth in the use of project techniques.

Computer software firms now are turning their attention to integrating their specialized project management packages (e.g., resource and cost packages). Emphasis is on all phases of project management—planning, scheduling, and controlling. Systems are now available to handle very large multiproject, multiresource project organizations. The construction industry has been working hard to develop total information systems designed for contractors. There will probably be spin-offs for other industries from this effort. Concurrent with the total information thrust has been the increased development of packages which offer more features. Graphics and precedence diagramming options are increasing in availability, as are interactive and on-line systems for the smaller project users. There is little doubt that computer-based project management systems will increase in use and in systems available. The most notable changes will take place in new packages for small computer systems. The Project Management Institute conducts a survey periodically and publishes a short description of the software packages included in their survey.[1,2] This is a valuable reference for those interested in the computer side of project management.

GRAPHICS

Bar charts have always been popular with managers. Generating bar charts is a very easy task for a computer, even for small ones, and most software packages include bar chart options. Drawing networks is a bit more complicated. Until recently, the plotting of networks was reserved for large computers hooked up to an expensive plotting device. The state of the art is developing quickly as the price of plotters continues to decrease. In the next few years exotic plotting routines using multiple colors will be available to a larger segment of project managers in both paper and television screen output.

PROFESSIONALISM

Project management appears to be a part of every manager's job. For example, it covers such fields as construction, engineering, forestry, data processing, production, accounting, marketing, research and development, and government administration.

The project management techniques available to these managers constitute a well-defined body of knowledge. A few leaders are suggesting curricula and professional certification for project managers similar to those found in the fields of accounting, data processing, production control, financial planning, etc. The implication behind all of this is that project mana-

---

1. "Computer Software Survey, 1980," Project Management Institute, Technology Committee, Box 43, Drexel Hill, Pennsylvania 19026.
2. Other surveys not in as great detail: "Comparing Commercially Available CPM/PERT Computer Programs," *Industrial Engineering*, April 1978, pp. 37-39; "Project Control Systems," Petersen, Perry. *Datamation*, June 1979. pp. 147-62.

gers represent a profession. The movement is not limited to the United States; Britain, France, Germany, Japan, Australia, Canada, and Brazil all have their own national organizations representing project managers. Europe has even created the organization called INTERNET to bring project managers from member countries together. In the United States the Project Management Institute has provided a forum in its annual meetings and its quarterly journal for those managers interested in project management.

Since project management is a part of almost every manager's job, its wide applicability ensures it a permanent place in management literature and as a necessary part of any manager's training.

CONCLUSIONS

This is an age of increased *accountability* for management at all levels in both the private and public sectors. Managers must be willing to make their decisions visible to top management and the public and be willing to be accountable for the outcomes of those decisions. The project management techniques available to managers today can greatly enhance decision making and coordination. A good project management information system provides the same information to management at all levels—either in detail or summary form; problems are visible to all and encourage cooperation among those responsible for completing the project on schedule. It seems certain that project managers will continue to use the improved techniques and information systems available. The key is to use them correctly.

Answers to Selected Exercises

2-2.

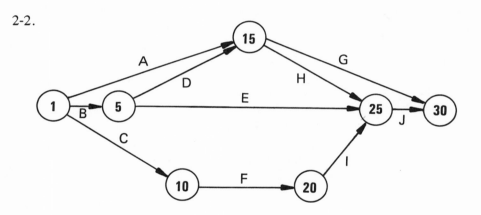

2-4.

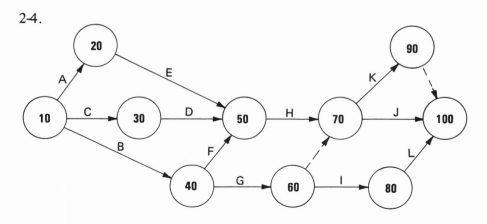

2-6.
(a)

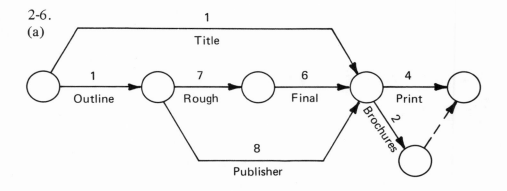

(b) 18 weeks

CHAPTER 3

3-2.

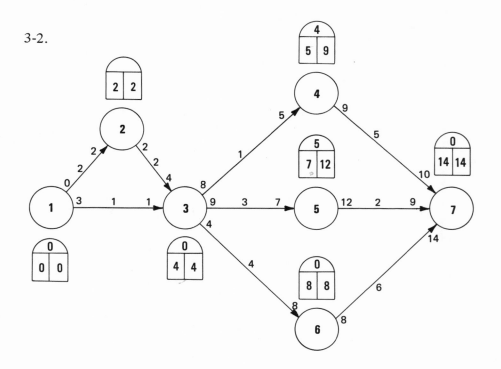

	EVENTS				ACTIVITIES					
#	E	L	Slack	#	ES	LS	EF	LF	Slack	Crit.
1	0	0	0	1–2	0	0	2	2	0	*
2	2	2	0	1–3	0	3	1	4	3	
3	4	4	0	2–3	2	2	4	4	0	*
4	5	9	4	3–4	4	8	5	9	4	
5	7	12	5	3–5	4	9	7	12	5	
6	8	8	0	3–6	4	4	8	8	0	*
7	14	14	0	4–7	5	9	10	14	4	
				5–7	7	12	9	14	5	
				6–7	8	8	14	14	0	*

3-4.

ACTIVITY TIMES

Activity	Duration	ES	LS	EF	LF	Slack	Crit.
1–2	3	0	2	3	5	2	
1–3	5	0	0	5	5	0	*
2–3	0	3	5	3	5	2	
3–4	1	5	10	6	11	5	
3–5	2	5	6	7	8	1	
3–6	4	5	5	9	9	0	*
4–7	3	6	11	9	14	5	
5–6	0	7	9	7	9	2	
5–7	6	7	8	13	14	1	
6–7	5	9	9	14	14	0	*

3-6.
(a,b)

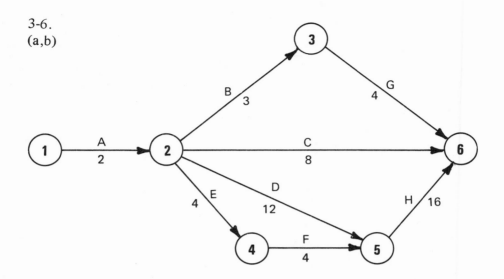

(c)

ACTIVITY TIMES

Activity ID		ES	LS	EF	LF	Slack
1-2	A	0	0	2	2	0
2-3	B	2	23	5	26	21
2-6	C	2	22	10	30	20
2-5	D	2	2	14	14	0
2-4	E	2	6	6	10	4
4-5	F	6	10	10	14	4
3-6	G	5	26	9	30	21
5-6	H	14	14	30	30	0

3-8.

(a)

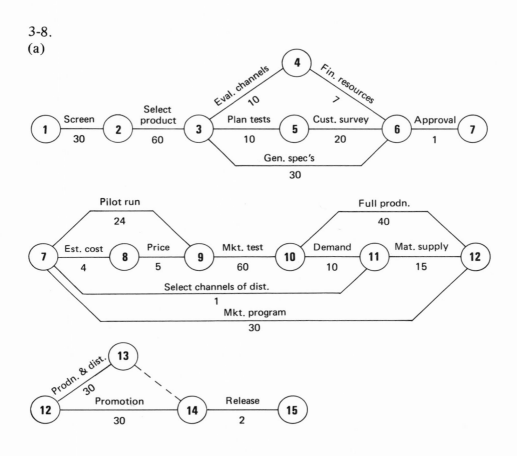

(b) 1,2,3,6,7,9,10,12,14,15
1,2,3,5,6,7,9,10,12,14,15
1,2,3,6,7,9,10,12,13,14,15
1,2,3,5,6,7,9,10,12,13,14,15

(c) 277

(d) (1) 0 days
(2) 13 days
(3) 94 days
(4) 0 days

CHAPTER 4

4-2.

TIME	19	TIME	17	TIME	16	TIME	15
Dir Cost	$210	Dir Cost	$250	Dir Cost	$310	Dir Cost	$400
CP	1,2,3,5	CP	1,2,3,5	CP	1,2,3,5	CP	1,2,3,5
			1,2,5		1,2,5		1,2,5
TIME	18		1,4,5		1,4,5		1,4,5
Dir Cost	$220	ACT CHGD	2-3,2-5	ACT CHGD	1-2,1-4	ACT CHGD	1-2,4-5
CP	1,2,5						
	1,2,3,5						
ACT CHGD	2-3						

DURATION	DIRECT COST	INDIRECT COST	TOTAL COST
19	$210	$200	$410
18	220	180	400 optimum
17	250	160	410
16	310	140	450
15	400	120	520

4-4.

DURATION	DIRECT COST	INDIRECT COST	TOTAL COST	ACTIVITIES CHANGED
27	$300	$300	$600	None
26	330	240	570	4-5
25	380	180	560 optimum	2-4
24	470	120	590	2-4,1-3
23	650	60	710	1-2,3-4
22	830	50	880	1-2,3-4

Take the incentive down to 25 time units; this is low cost and optimum (with or without the incentive). The incentive lowers costs to $560 for 26 time units, $540 for 25, and $560 for 24.

4-6.

DURATION	DIRECT COST	INDIRECT COST	TOTAL COST	ACTIVITIES CHANGED
19	$590	$700	$1290	None
18	610	600	1210	3–6
17	660	500	1160	4–7,6–8
16	720	400	1120 optimum	1–2
15	890	300	1190	2–3, 4–6, 7–8
14	1160	200	1360	2–3,2–4

4-8.

DURATION	DIRECT COST	INDIRECT COST	TOTAL COST	ACTIVITIES CHANGED
14	$36	$25	$61	None
13	39	20	59	3–5
12	45	15	60	2–3,2–4
11	55	10	65	1–2,4–5
				Buy back 2–4

CHAPTER 5

5-2.

TIME PERIOD	ACTIVITIES SCHEDULED (UNSCHEDULED)		UPDATED ACTIVITIES			
0–1	Sched.	1–2,1–5	None			
1–2	None		None			
2–3	Sched.	5–9	None			
3–4	Sched.	2–3	2–4	ES=4, SI=5		
4–5	None		2–4	ES=5, SI=4	4–7	ES=10, SI=4
5–6	Sched.	3–6	2–4	ES=6, SI=3	3–4	ES=6, SI=4
			4–7	ES=11, SI=3		
6–7	None		2–4	ES=7, SI=2	3–4	ES=7, SI=3
			4–7	ES=12, SI=2		

TIME PERIOD	ACTIVITIES SCHEDULED (UNSCHEDULED)		UPDATED ACTIVITIES		
7-8	None		2-4 ES=8, SI=1	3-4 ES=8, SI=2	
			4-7 ES=13, SI=1		
8-9	None		2-4 ES=9, SI=0	3-4 ES=9, SI=1	
			4-7 ES=14, SI=0	9-10 ES=9, SI=5	
9-10	Sched.	2-4,6-7,3-4	6-8 ES=10, SI=5	8-10 ES=12, SI=5	
			9-10 ES=10, SI=4		
10-11	None		6-8 ES=11, SI=4	8-10 ES=13, SI=4	
			9-10 ES=11, SI=3		
11-12	None		6-8 ES=12, SI=3	8-10 ES=14, SI=3	
			9-10 ES=12, SI=2		
12-13	None		6-8 ES=13, SI=2	8-10 ES=15, SI=2	
			9-10 ES=13, SI=1		
13-14	Sched.	9-10	6-8 ES=14, SI=1	8-10 ES=16, SI=1	
14-15	Unsched.	9-10	9-10 ES=15, SI=-1	8-10 ES=17, SI=0	
	Sched.	4-7	6-8 ES=15, SI=0		
15-16	Sched.	9-10,6-8	7-10 ES=16, SI=-1		
16-17	None		7-10 ES=17, SI=-2		
17-18	Sched.	7-10	8-10 ES=18, SI=-1		
18-19	None		8-10 ES=19, SI=-2		
19-20	Sched.	8-10	None		

The completion date has been extended from 18 to 20 time units. The following activities are critical: 1-2, 2-4, 3-6, 4-7, 6-7, 6-8, 7-10, 8-10, 9-10.

An alternative schedule (to "unscheduling") is presented below:

TIME PERIOD	ACTIVITIES SCHEDULED (UNSCHEDULED)		UPDATED ACTIVITIES	
14-15	Sched.	6-8	4-7 ES=15, SI=-1	7-10 ES=16, SI=-1
15-16	None		4-7 ES=16, SI=-2	7-10 ES=17, SI=-2
16-17	Sched.	4-7	8-10 ES=17, SI=0	
17-18	Sched.	7-10,8-10		

The completion date is extended to 20 time units.

5-4.

TIME PERIOD	ACTIVITIES SCHEDULED (UNSCHEDULED)		UPDATED ACTIVITIES					
0-1	Sched.	1-2,1-3,1-4	None					
1-2	None		None					
2-3	Sched.	4-8	4-7	ES=3,	SI=8			
3-4	Unsched.	4-8						
	Sched.	2-6,2-5	4-7	ES=4,	SI=7	4-8	ES=4,	SI=5
4-5	Sched.	3-7,4-8	4-7	ES=5,	SI=6			
5-6	Sched.	5-9	4-7	ES=6,	SI=5			
6-7	None		4-7	ES=7,	SI=4	8-10	ES=7,	SI=6
7-8	Sched.	4-7	8-10	ES=8,	SI=5			
8-9	Sched.	6-9,6-7,8-10	None					
9-10	None		None					
10-11	Sched.	7-10	None					
11-12	None		None					
12-13	None		9-10	ES=13,	SI=-1			
13-14	Sched.	9-10						

The project duration has been extended from 15 to 16 time units. The efficiency of the schedule is 80% for slippage and 83.9% for resource.

$$\text{Slippage} = 1.0 - \left(\frac{\text{Sched. dur.} - \text{Plan dur.}}{\text{Plan dur.}} \right) \qquad \text{Resource} = U_j = \frac{\sum\limits_{i=0}^{i=D} R_i}{D \times L}$$

Slippage = 1.0 - [(16-15)/15]
        = 93%

Resource = 94/(16×7)
      = 83.9%

<u>**CHAPTER 6**</u>

6-2.
A-1.

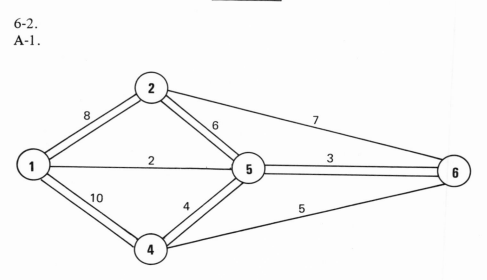

A-2.

FINANCIAL REQUIREMENTS SCHEDULE

Activity	Dura-tion	Bud-get	ST	1	2	3	4	5	6	7	8	9	10	11	12	13	14	15	16	17
1–2	8	48	0	6	6	6	6	6	6	6	6									
1–4	10	40	0	4	4	4	4	4	4	4	4	4	4							
1–5	2	14	0	7	7															
2–5	6	30	8									5	5	5	5	5	5			
2–6	7	21	8									3	3	3	3	3	3	3		
4–5	4	28	10											7	7	7	7			
4–6	5	40	10											8	8	8	8	8		
5–6	3	27	14															9	9	9
PERIOD TOTAL				17	17	10	10	10	10	10	10	12	12	23	23	23	23	20	9	9
CUMULATIVE TOTAL				17	34	44	54	64	74	84	94	106	118	141	164	187	210	230	239	248

6-2.
B-1.

CURRENT PROJECT COST STATUS REPORT

ACT	ORI DUR	ORI BGT	1	2	3	4	5	6	7	8	9	ACT TO DATE	10	11	12	13	14	15	16	17	18	19	TOTAL TO COMPLETE
1-2	8	48	6/6	6/6	6/6	6/6	6/6	6/6	6/6	6/6		48											48
1-4	10	40	10/5	16/8	8/4	8/4	4/2	6/3	2/1	8/4	8/4	70	6	4									80
1-5	2	14	5/7	5/7								10											10
2-5	6	30								6/5		6	6	6	6	6	6						36
2-6	7	21								2/3		2	2	2	2	2	2	2					14
4-5	4	28													7	7	7	7					28
4-6	5	40													8	8	8	8	8				40
5-6	3	27																	9	9	9	9	36
TOTAL		248	21	27	14	14	10	12	8	14	16	136	14	12	23	23	23	17	17	9	9	9	292
CUM. TOTAL			21	48	62	76	86	98	106	120	136		150	162	185	208	231	248	265	274	283	292	
EARN. BUDGET			18	21	10	10	8	9	7	10	12												
CUM. EAR. BUDGET			18	39	49	59	67	76	83	93	105												

Legend: Actual / Earned

PROJECT COST SUMMARY REPORT

Work Performed To Date

Activity	Earned Budget Value	Actual Cost	Over/ Underrun
1-2	48	48	---
1-4	35	70	(35)
1-5	14	10	4
2-5	5	6	(1)
2-6	3	2	1
4-5			
4-6			
5-6			
TOTAL	$105	$136	$(31)

Total Cost At Completion

Activity	Original Cost Budget	Latest Revised	Over/ Underrun
1-2	48	48	---
1-4	40	80	(40)
1-5	14	10	4
2-5	30	36	(6)
2-6	21	14	7
4-5	28	28	---
4-6	40	40	---
5-6	27	36	(9)
TOTAL	$248	$292	$(44)

6-2.

B-2. Omitted

B-3. The project duration has been extended to 19 periods. Since activity 1-4 is very nearly completed, it is highly probable that it will continue to be late one period and the estimated $80 completion cost will occur—you have actually spent $70 already. Activities 2-5 and 5-6 hold potential for cutting back on latest cost estimates. What is the cause of the change in time for activity 5-6? Your actual dollars spent are $31 over earned and $30 over budget. If things continue with no changes, you will be over $44 (000) and two periods late.

CHAPTER 8

8-2.

(a,b) Expected times and variances for activities:

ACTIVITY	TIME	VARIANCE	ACTIVITY	TIME	VARIANCE
1-2	20	4	4-8	13	9
1-5	30	0	5-10	26	4
1-6	73	25	6-11	35	25
1-7	26	4	7-9	60	100
2-3	30	25	8-10	20	9
2-4	7	1	9-11	22	4
3-4	15	1	10-11	16	1

(c) Project duration is 114 days.

(d) Probability of completing in 112 days:

$$Z = (112 - 114)/\sqrt{49} = -2/7 = -.286; \text{ therefore } p \approx .40$$

Completing in 116 days:

$$Z = (116 - 114)/\sqrt{49} = +2/7 = +.286; \text{ therefore } p \approx .60$$

(e) Probability of completing 7-9 by day 90:

$$Z = (90 - 86)/\sqrt{104} = \text{approx. } +4/10 = +.40; \text{ therefore } p \approx .65$$

8-4. Probability of completing in 29 weeks:

$$Z = (29 - 31)/\sqrt{20 + 10 + 6} = -2/6 = -.333; \text{ therefore } p \approx .37$$

Appendix

Number	Squared	Square Root	Number	Squared	Square Root	Number	Squared	Square Root	Number	Squared	Square Root
1	1	1.0	26	676	5.0	51	2601	7.1	76	5776	8.7
2	4	1.4	27	729	5.1	52	2704	7.2	77	5929	8.77
3	9	1.7	28	784	5.2	53	2809	7.28	78	6084	8.8
4	16	2.0	29	841	5.3	54	2916	7.3	79	6241	8.88
5	25	2.2	30	900	5.4	55	3025	7.4	80	6400	8.9
6	36	2.4	31	961	5.5	56	3136	7.48	81	6561	9.0
7	49	2.6	32	1024	5.6	57	3249	7.5	82	6724	9.05
8	64	2.8	33	1089	5.7	58	3364	7.6	83	6889	9.1
9	81	3.0	34	1156	5.8	59	3481	7.68	84	7056	9.16
10	100	3.1	35	1225	5.9	60	3600	7.7	85	7225	9.2
11	121	3.3	36	1296	6.0	61	3721	7.8	86	7396	9.27
12	144	3.4	37	1369	6.08	62	3844	7.87	87	7569	9.3
13	169	3.6	38	1444	6.1	63	3969	7.9	88	7744	9.38
14	196	3.7	39	1521	6.2	64	4096	8.0	89	7921	9.4
15	225	3.8	40	1600	6.3	65	4225	8.06	90	8100	9.48
16	256	4.0	41	1681	6.4	66	4356	8.1	91	8281	9.5
17	289	4.1	42	1764	6.48	67	4489	8.18	92	8464	9.59
18	324	4.2	43	1849	6.5	68	4624	8.2	93	8649	9.6
19	361	4.3	44	1936	6.6	69	4761	8.3	94	8836	9.69
20	400	4.4	45	2025	6.7	70	4900	8.36	95	9025	9.7
21	441	4.5	46	2116	6.78	71	5041	8.4	96	9216	9.79
22	484	4.6	47	2209	6.8	72	5184	8.48	97	9409	9.8
23	529	4.7	48	2304	6.9	73	5329	8.5	98	9604	9.89
24	576	4.8	49	2401	7.0	74	5476	8.6	99	9801	9.94
25	625	5.0	50	2500	7.07	75	5625	8.66	100	10000	10.00

SQUARES OF SELECTED NUMBERS

Number	Squared	Square Root	Number	Squared	Square Root	Number	Squared	Square Root	Number	Squared	Square Root
1.0	1.0	1.0	2.0	4.00	1.41	3.0	9.00	1.73	4.0	16.00	2.0
1.1	1.21	1.04	2.1	4.41	1.44	3.1	9.61	1.76	4.2	17.64	2.03
1.2	1.44	1.09	2.2	4.84	1.48	3.2	10.24	1.78	4.4	19.36	2.09
1.3	1.69	1.14	2.3	5.29	1.51	3.3	10.89	1.81	4.6	21.16	2.1
1.4	1.96	1.18	2.4	5.76	1.54	3.4	11.56	1.84	4.8	23.04	2.19
1.5	2.25	1.22	2.5	6.25	1.58	3.5	12.25	1.87	5.0	25.00	2.23
1.6	2.56	1.26	2.6	6.76	1.61	3.6	12.56	1.89	5.2	27.04	2.28
1.7	2.89	1.3	2.7	7.29	1.64	3.7	13.69	1.92	5.4	29.16	2.32
1.8	3.24	1.34	2.8	7.84	1.67	3.8	14.44	1.94	5.6	31.36	2.36
1.9	3.61	1.37	2.9	8.41	1.7	3.9	15.21	1.97	5.8	33.64	2.4

SQUARE OF A NUMBER

To square a number means to multiply the number by itself. For example, the square of the number 5 is $5 \times 5 = 25$.

FIND THE SQUARE OF A NUMBER

For example, you want the square of the number 5. You look under the column "Number" until you find the number 5. Then you will find the answer in the column to the right.

SQUARE ROOT OF A NUMBER

To find the square root of a number, find the number which, when multiplied times itself, will equal the number under the square root radical ($\sqrt{}$). For example, the square root of 9 ($\sqrt{9}$). The number 3 when multiplied times itself is $3 \times 3 = 9$; hence, the square root of 9 is 3.

FIND THE SQUARE ROOT OF A NUMBER

For example, you want the square root of the number 9. You look under the column "Number" until you find the number 9. Then you will find the number in the column "Square Root" directly to the right of the number.

Index

239